INSIGHT COMPACT GUIDES

NOR

CW00324042

Compact Guide: Normandy is the ultimate quick-reference guide to this delightful region of France. It tells you everything you need to know about the region's attractions, from its cathedrals to its châteaux, from its Calvados to its Camembert.

This is just one title in *Apa Publications'* new series of pocket-sized, easy-to-use guidebooks intended for the independent-minded traveller. Based on an award-winning formula pioneered in Germany, *Compact Guides* pride themselves on being up-to-date and authoritative. They are in essence mini travel encyclopedias, designed to be comprehensive yet portable, both readable and reliable.

Star Attractions

An instant reference to some of Normandy's most popular tourist attractions to help you on your way.

Cathédrale Notre-Dame p19

Aître de St-Maclou p21

Etretat p29

Honfleur Vieux Port p46

Livarot p50

Calvados p53

Abbaye aux Hommes, Caen p59

Omaha Beach p63

Anse de Vauville p71

Bayeux p64

Mont St-Michel p73

NORMANDY

Introduction

Places

Culture

Leisure

Practical Information

Normandy – Land of Cheese and Calvados

Ramshackle cow sheds; Norman and Gothic churches and castle ruins sit harmoniously together; doves fly from dovecotes as strong as castle walls; thatched roofs are topped with irises; cattle rest under pink apple blossom; sheep graze on salty meadows at the edge of cliffs which drop abruptly into the sea; picture postcard half-timbered villages underneath the fluttering flags of Calvados and market stalls weighed down with heart-shaped cheeses. Who could ignore this corner of Europe?

It is easy to be drawn to a region which appeals so immediately to the heart. Where feelings and emotions run high, distances seem to matter little. Perhaps this is what makes it so easy to get close to Normandy. Over 600km (375 miles) of contrasting coastline includes beaches as flat and as safe as a bath-towel, alabaster chalk cliffs as high and as steep as the side of a skyscraper, wind-blown sand dunes, fishing villages and small ports with lobster pots piled high and luminous buoys beyond the quayside. Weather-beaten fishermen in berets sitting in the sun mending their nets; wooden boxes brim with scallops, whelks and oysters. The sea, here called *la Manche*, does not end at the beach in Normandy – it makes its mark on the whole region.

Normandy appeals to the heart

Between sailings

5

Its presence is felt on the thinly populated farmland of the Cotentin peninsula, surrounded on three sides by the English Channel, and equally on the monotonous Pays de Caux plateau. It breathes its salty breath through the wooded river valleys of the Bresle, Orne and Vire. Even the ancient cathedral city of Rouen, the region's biggest city some 110km (70 miles) from the coast, cannot escape the ceaseless tidal ebb and flow.

What makes Normandy so unique is not just its proximity to the sea. It is a region of fascinating contrasts. In the remotest regions amid fields of cauliflowers and beech hedges, suddenly there are fortresses, castles and ruined monasteries – all of which have played their part in 2,000 years of changing fortunes. It is a history shaped by Roman empire builders, pillaging Vikings, Norman dukes and French monarchs, by periods of pomp and splendour as well as by the dark days of plagues and wretched wars. Many a tiny village has found itself on the tourist itinerary thanks to its majestic Renaissance château, but visit the local *bar-tabac* afterwards and you will find yourself sharing the counter with the locals in their wellington boots who have called in on their way home from the fields.

Tension exists and it is not just between agriculture and art, yesterday and today. Fascinating paradoxes and contradictions are very much in evidence – and they are not always positive.

The beach at Cabourg

Position and topography

In a geographical sense, Normandy can justifiably be described as on the 'edge of Europe'. This region in the northwest of France extends from the densely populated Paris basin to the English Channel. It is bordered to the northeast by Picardy and to the southwest by Brittany. The 600km (375 mile) coastline is an unmistakable symbol of Normandy, characterised by the spectacular chalk cliffs at Etretat in the Pays de Caux, the inviting flat, sandy beaches in the *département* of Calvados and the fissured rocky coast and miles of sandy beaches on the Cotentin peninsula. With a surface area of 30,000sq km (11,600sq miles), Normandy is on a par with Belgium.

Normandy's geological sub-structure and topography are greatly varied. In Lower (Basse) Normandy, west of the imaginary Alençon-Valognes line, the region together with Brittany forms part of the granite Armorican Massif. Hills such as those in the Suisse Normande (Swiss Normandy) rise to about 400m (1,300ft). Eastern or Upper (Haute) Normandy, on the other hand, is part of the wide Paris basin and consists of a flat plateau with sedimentary chalk and limestone reaching no more then 200m (650ft). The rivers Seine, Eure, Orne, Dives, Risle and Bresle flow through the region, with the Seine an important artery for river transport. On its banks lies the historic capital of Rouen and the city centre, largely rebuilt since 1945, is only a few metres away. Ships up to 10,000 tons use the large port complex.

A number of islands lie off the coast of the Cotentin peninsula, which extends north into the English Channel. The Channel Islands of Guernsey, Jersey and Alderney are of course British, the Iles Chausey, 17km (10 miles) from Granville, are French.

And what about the *bocage normand*? This term is used to describe the rural terrain to the east of Avranches. There, fields, meadows and orchards are often separated by ancient hedgerows, with narrow roads and tracks passing between. For centuries, these trees have protected the land from wind erosion and also provided the farmers with firewood. Over the centuries, the paths have worn down and the tips of the trees and bushes along many of the verges meet in the middle.

6

The chalk cliffs of Etretat

Flower market in Rouen

Climate

The mild, moist sea air provides the rainfall that gives the landscape its rich colour. The average temperature is 11–12°C (52–54°F) and the effects of the Gulf Stream ensure that, winter or summer, the mercury levels never register extremes and the exotic plants in the Parc Emmanuel-Liais in Cherbourg prove the point. On average there are fewer than 20 days of frost a year. In the interior, in the *bocage normand* for example, greater temperature fluctuations occur. Precipitation amounts to about 800mm (31in), most of which falls in the autumn and winter. The best time to visit Normandy is in July and August, but autumn can also be very pleasant.

Nature and environment

Normandy is no more immune to change than other regions of France. Many barn doors have been bolted for good in the last few years and dairies have had to close because of low profits. Many of these have now been converted into *ferme-auberges*. Young people have been turning their backs on the country life for decades.

The deer are taking over

The 'green' image of Normandy has been tarnished, as the Seine has become the second most polluted river in France. On the coast, nuclear power stations and nuclear waste reprocessing plants are proof that the hi-tech age has caught up with the region. Nevertheless, there are some areas where great efforts have been made to preserve the natural environment. The Parc Naturel Régional de Brotonne extends along the Seine Valley from the mouth of the river to Le Trait. The western end of the region is known as the *Marais Vernier*, an unspoilt natural landscape in marshland close to the Seine estuary. Lying between St-Sauveur-le-Vicomte in the west and Treviers in the east, the Parc Régional du Marais du Cotentin et du Bessin extends over typical *bocage normand* as well as the marshland close to the Baie des Veys where the Vire, Sèves, Tortonne and Douve flow into the sea.

Population

Normandy has retained its rural character despite the three major conurbations of Rouen, Le Havre and Caen. The total population of the region is 3.15 million of which 1.73 million live in Haute Normandie and 1.42 million live in Basse Normandie. The term 'Norman' derives from the Viking 'Norsemen' who invaded the region in the 9th century and later took control when the Viking leader Rollo became the first Duke of Normandy.

Three of a kind

Customs

Normandy is traditionally a region of farmers and fishermen, but the truth is that this part of France, like everywhere else, has had to keep up with the changes in society, and in the course of time, customs and traditions have been adapted or have simply died away. In some parts, however, the old ways have been retained and one such example is the weekly market, where farmers and local traders sell their produce directly to the community.

Pilgrimages to Normandy's many shrines have also continued. Mont St-Michel has long been a destination for pilgrims and, even during the Hundred Years' War, the feast of Archangel Michael was always celebrated on 29 September, drawing pilgrims who bought safe-conduct to the rocky island. Homage is now paid to St Michael on the Sunday nearest to that date.

Traditional head gear

Men, women and children still sometimes wear traditional costumes for certain festivals. On special occasions in the *département* of Calvados, women and girls can still be seen in long dresses and pointed hats. In some communities, hierarchical brotherhoods dedicated to a particular saint perform public ceremonies with banners, emblems and costumes. These organisations date from the 12th century when Brothers of Mercy attended to the funerals of plague victims. In Bernay, a brotherhood organises a procession every May.

Economy

The economy of Normandy cannot be described as a homogeneous unit, as many differences exist between the various *départements* or 'sub-regions'. Basse Normandie is oriented more to agriculture than Haute Normandie, where roughly 120,000 people or 24 percent of the working population are employed in industry (food, electrical goods, electronics and motor manufacturing), in line with the French average. In western Normandy, mainly the *département* of Manche, cattle and horse rearing and arable farming predominate. Dairy farming is important in the Pays d'Auge, where the world famous Camembert, Pont-l'Evêque and Livarot cheeses are made. Just under 20 percent of the working population are employed on the land in the *départements* of Manche and Orne, way above the national average of 6 per cent. A clearer picture of rural Normandy can be drawn from the fact that the region is responsible for 15 percent of the total French milk production. The Seine Valley and the Le Havre estuary are the major industrial regions. The port of Rouen benefits from the fact that it is only 110km (70 miles) from the English Channel and is accessible to deep-sea vessels. Le Havre is a major port for oil and oil-related imports and follows closely behind Marseille as France's busiest port. Chemical processing plays an important part in the local economy.

The market at Rouen

A prize specimen

Administration

Strictly speaking, Normandy, one of 22 French regions, is made up of the two sub-regions of Basse Normandie and Haute Normandie. The former consists of the *départements* of Calvados, Manche and Orne and the latter of Seine-Maritime and Eure. Since 1983, the joint region of Normandy has enjoyed decentralised responsibilities for the economy, education and training. At that time, all French regions acquired a degree of autonomy with a democratically elected council.

Norman tongue-twisters

Criquebec, Hambye, Houlgate, Ouistreham – Norman place-names which many French, let alone foreign visitors, have difficulty pronouncing. The reason is simple: these names are derived from Nordic, the language of the Viking invaders. From the beginning of the 10th century, when Normandy fell to Viking rule, the language of the Scandinavian settlers started to merge with the Latin-influenced French language. Some 1,000 years later, only place-names betray the Nordic roots of many of Normandy's early inhabitants. The *-fleur* ending, for example, meant 'flood' or 'fjord' and can be found in such names as Fiquefleur and Honfleur. The final syllable *-bec*, as in Orbec or Criquebec means stream and *-beuf*, as in Daubeuf and Lindebeuf, means house.

A windy day in Houlgate

Many other place-names have resulted from a combination of Scandinavian Christian names and the French ending *-ville*. This final syllable occurs in more than 30 percent of all place-names, well above the average for the whole of France. Besneville and Bierville, for example, are derived from Björn, Rauville and Rouville from Hrolf, Veauville and Vauville from Valr and Touffrainville from Thorfrod.

9

One difficult name to pronounce is Ouistreham, a coastal town on the Côte de Nacre. Etymologists have concluded that *Ouistre* almost certainly comes from the Anglo-Saxon word *ouster* meaning east, while *ham* is a Germanic suffix for a small settlement or farmhouse. In French the word *hameau* means a small village or hamlet.

Half-timbered house in Honfleur

Historical Highlights

58–51BC Roman troops under Julius Caesar conquer the resident celtic tribes in the northwest of what is now France, and establish their regional capital at Rotomagus (Rouen).

52BC The Romans found the towns of Harfleur and Lisieux.

2nd century AD Christianity spreads throughout Normandy.

260 St Mellon is first bishop of Rouen.

486 Normandy conquered by Frankish Merovingian empire under King Clovis.

7th century The first monasteries established in Jumièges and Fontanelle in the Seine Valley.

708 Abbey of Mont St-Michel founded.

820 The first Viking raids up the Seine Valley.

841 Vikings invade Normandy, plundering the abbey at Jumièges.

911 Rollo, the Viking leader, and the French king, Charles le Simple, sign the Treaty of St-Clair-sur-Epte to found the Duchy of Normandy.

933 Accession of William Longsword; monastery rebuilding begins.

1027 Birth of William the Conqueror. By 1047, he has succeeded in overcoming his political rivals.

1066 William defeats Harold at the Battle of Hastings and becomes king of England.

1180–1223 Philippe-Auguste, king of France, reinforces castles in Normandy.

1195 Richard Lionheart, king of England, builds Château Gaillard.

1204 Château Gaillard captured by Philippe-Auguste, who goes on to conquer all Normandy except for the Isles Normandes (Channel Islands) and the duchy is united with the French crown.

1315 Normandy awarded provincial status.

1337 The English king Edward III revives his claim to the French throne, marking the beginning of the Hundred Years' War.

1346 English victorious at the Battle of Crécy.

1415 Henry V of England arrives at Honfleur and takes all Normandy.

1431 Accused of sorcery and heresy, Joan of Arc is burned at the stake in Rouen.

1437 Caen University is founded.

1453 All of France, except for Calais, is back in French hands.

1469 The French monarchy gives up the title to the duchy of Normandy.

1517 Le Havre founded by François I.

1572 The St Batholomew's Day Massacre of Protestant Hugenots; 500 killed in Rouen.

1598 The Edict of Nantes grants the Huguenots religious and civil liberties.

1608 On his third voyage to North America, Samuel de Champlain founds the Canadian city of Quebec.

1630–36 Serious plague epidemic strikes Normandy.

1685 Louis XIV, the Sun King, revokes the Edict of Nantes and begins the persecution of the Huguenots.

1692 Fleet sets sail from La Hougue to restore James II to the English throne, and is disastrously defeated.

1756–63 Seven Years' War with England.

1789–92 The French Revolution leads to the First Republic. Monasteries abandoned and destroyed. Normandy ceases to exist as a province.

1804–14 First Empire is established under Napoleon Bonaparte.

1830 Charles X goes into exile in Cherbourg.

1843 Completion of railway line from Paris to Rouen.

1848 Rioting in Rouen. King Louis-Philippe leaves Honfleur for exile in Britain.

1848–52 Second Empire.

1856 *Madame Bovary* by Gustave Flaubert published, outraging the citizens of Rouen.

1850 Guy de Maupassant, the great Norman writer, is born near Fécamp.

1870–1 Upper Normandy occupied during Franco-Prussian war.

1914–18 World War I.

1920 Joan of Arc canonised and becomes patron saint of France.

1932 The ocean liner *Normandie* breaks transatlantic records.

1939–45 World War II.

1940 France capitulates to Germany and all of France is occupied. Towns and cities in Haute Normandie ravaged by fire.

1942 Canadian attempt to create a bridgehead in Dieppe fails with huge loss of life.

1944 'Operation Overlord' begins at daybreak on 6 June (D-Day). A co-ordinated landing of allied forces takes place at several locations along the Normandy coast. Bitter fighting culminates in the Falaise Pocket, 22 August.

1957 France becomes a founder member of the European Economic Community.

1976 A deep-sea harbour for supertankers constructed at Cap d'Antifer.

1982 The Oscar Niemeyer Cultural Centre opened in Le Havre.

1994 Completion of the Pont de Normandie Seine crossing between Le Havre and Honfleur.

The Hundred Years' War

Dynastic feuds have frequently wreaked death and destruction upon innocent subjects, but for a marriage to precipitate a war between two nations which lasted for over a hundred years, was an exceptional case even by European standards. The momentous marriage bond was struck in 1152 at the church of St-Pierre in Lisieux when Henry II, the Plantagenet duke of Normandy, wed Eleanor of Aquitaine. Two years later, Henry was crowned king of England. As a consequence, not just England and Normandy, but also large parts of western France, such as Aquitaine, Anjou, Gascony and Brittany, were united under one throne. The Angevin Empire remained intact until Phillip II (1180–1223) captured parts of the empire, including Normandy (1204), for France.

Almost 200 years after the Lisieux marriage, the English king Edward III set about re-uniting the English and French crowns under his rule. With the death of Charles IV in 1328, the Capetian dynasty ended. As nephew of the former French king, Edward made claims on the French throne, thereby precipitating the Hundred Years' War (1337–1453). Of those 116 years, however, only 53 were in fact years of war, the rest were relatively peaceful. From what was initially a feudal power struggle among the Capetian pretenders, a bitter war between England and France developed and Normandy was the main battleground.

No other people suffered as much as a result of this feud between London and Paris. About one third of the total population died during those 116 years. Civilians suffered badly at the hands of the English who for the first time deployed cannons in the Battle of Crécy (1346). As well as the immediate effects of the war, the rural population suffered from the devastation of their land and from marauding brigands. Soon afterwards, a plague originating in Asia struck Europe, developing into one of the worst catastrophes ever to affect the western world.

Under the leadership of Joan of Arc, the Maid of Orléans, French troops won significant victories over the English who were eventually expelled. When the Hundred Years' War came to an end in 1453, political and social life had undergone dramatic changes. The English threat had, in fact, united the French people into one nation. Furthermore, a modern system of taxation, a professional army and an elementary civil service had been created – the basic elements for the absolutist state, which was later to be realised.

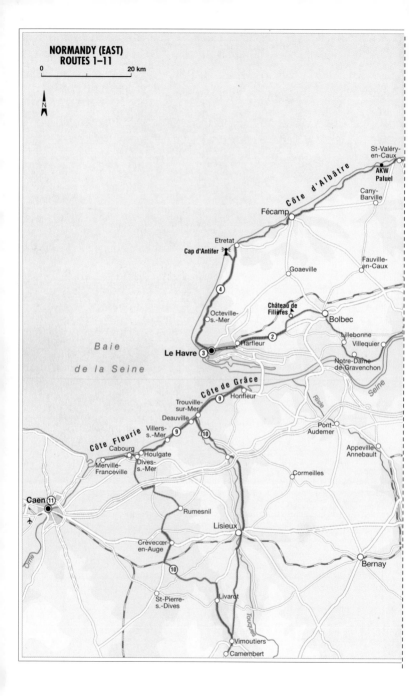

NORMANDY (EAST)
ROUTES 1–11

0   20 km

N

St-Valéry-
en-Caux

AKW
Paluel

Côte d'Albâtre

Cany-
Barville

Fécamp

Etretat

Fauville-
en-Caux

Cap d'Antifer

Goaeville

④

Château de
Filières

Bolbec

Octeville-
s.-Mer

Lillebonne

Villequier

Harfleur

②

Notre-Dame-
de-Gravenchon

Le Havre ③

Seine

Baie

de la Seine

Côte de Grâce

Honfleur

⑨

Risle

Trouville-
sur-Mer

Deauville

⑨

Villers-
s.-Mer

⑩

Pont-
Audemer

Côte Fleurie

Cabourg

Houlgate

Dives-
s.-Mer

Appeville-
Annebault

Merville-
Franceville

Cormeilles

Caen ⑪

Rumesnil

Lisieux

Crèvecœur-
en-Auge

Bernay

⑩

Orne

St-Pierre-
s.-Dives

Livarot

Touques

Vimoutiers

Camembert

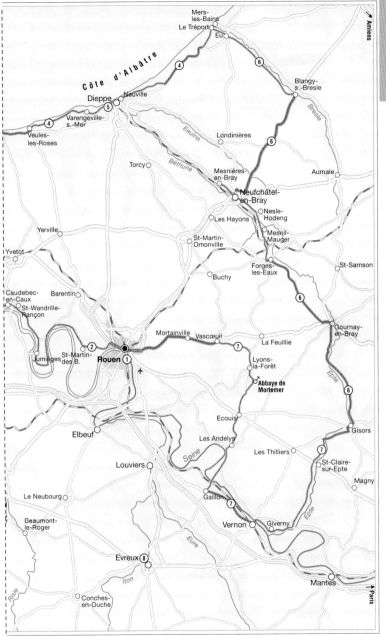

Place du Vieux-Marché

Route 1

★★ Rouen: a peep-hole into the Middle Ages

As the sun sets over the Atlantic, the Middle Ages appears to return to Rouen's old town centre of cobbled streets and gabled half-timbered houses. Doorways and shadowy corners look even darker in the dim light of the wrought-iron lanterns and when the clock tower chimes, the heart of the town could easily be mistaken for the film set of *The Three Musketeers* – but with the difference that, in Normandy's principal city, the half-timbered houses with their centuries-old facades, the Gothic church with its ornate towers and the solid Renaissance palace are not just a backdrop, but the stuff of history, architectural gems which have survived both dreadful misfortune and artistic and economic prosperity.

Rouen's centre of narrow alleys and weathered facades, its crumbling plaster and soaring Gothic towers will cap-

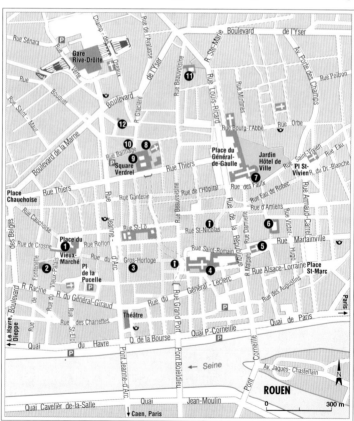

tivate you as soon as you cross from the modern ring road lined by functional but dull office blocks to the old town, a place that rouses heart and soul.

From the surrounding hillsides with their famous viewpoints such as the Basilique de Bonsecours or the suburb of Canteleu, the sea of roofs and towers could be any French city. But once immersed in the old heart of this Norman metropolis, then history overtakes you as if the Middle Ages had never ended.

Baguettes are best eaten fresh

Rouen is linked by rail to most major French cities. About 20 trains per day run between Rouen and Paris and the 139-km (86-mile) journey takes about 75 minutes. A scheduled bus service connects Rouen with most tourist destinations in the region.

History

The most famous event in the history of Rouen is the burning of Joan of Arc at the stake in 1431, but the city's history extends much further back than that – to before the Christian era. With its sand-banks and islands, this crossing-point on the Seine was settled by Gauls of the Veliocasse tribe. The settlement was named 'Rotomagus' by Julius Caesar's army who conquered it around 58–51BC. The town developed quickly and in 260 Bishop Mellon chose it as his first seat. In subsequent centuries the town continued to grow until the arrival of the Vikings in 841 brought its period of prosperity to an end. By the beginning of the 10th century, however, a community had been re-established there. Under the Treaty of St-Clair-sur-Epte (911), which created the Duchy of Normandy, Rollo, the Viking leader, chose Rouen as his capital and set about building a port.

The French king Phillip II conquered Normandy in 1204 and united it with France, but it was not until 1450, after the Hundred Years' War when the English were finally expelled, that Rouen and the rest of Normandy became a part of France again.

Rouen's golden age followed, lasting until the beginning of the Wars of Religion in 1562. The church of St-Maclou was built then in Flamboyant style as well as the cathedral's Tour de Beurre (Butter Tower). Under the influence of Rouen's Archbishop Georges I d'Amboise, late Gothic was succeeded by Italian Renaissance, a style which marked many of the town's secular buildings. A number of faience factories and weaving mills were built in the town, helping to create a busy and important industrial centre, and at the same time Rouen was emerging as a major port. Maritime travel was just starting to increase contact between trading nations at opposite ends of the globe. However, the Wars of Religion (1562–98)

17

Cobbled alleys

The cathedral's Butter Tower

and the Thirty Years' War (1618–48) had an adverse effect on Rouen's prosperity. The Revocation of the Edict of Nantes in 1685, which resulted in the Huguenots, who were mainly merchants and traders fleeing abroad, added to the town's decline. But with the invention in the 18th century of new machines for the textile industry and new materials, the town's fortunes were reversed. In 1843 the railway network was extended to include Rouen and the port complex was enlarged.

German troops occupied Haute Normandie during the Franco-Prussian War (1870–71), but it was World War II which inflicted most damage on Rouen. Almost the whole of the old town, as well as large parts of the industrial quarter, was destroyed. After the reconstruction and restoration of large parts of the old centre and the development of new housing estates and office blocks such as the *Cité Administrative* on the other side of the river, Rouen's population has grown to 380,000 and it is now the largest and most important industrial city in Normandy.

The Old Town

The Old Town, Rouen's window on to the past, lies on the north bank of the Seine. It is undoubtedly best to visit it on foot and in any case, car parking space is at a premium. Allow about 3 hours for this journey back into the Middle Ages. Add more time for visiting museums.

Display of oysters at the Place du Vieux-Marché

The ★ **Place du Vieux-Marché ❶**. A 20-m (65-ft) cross marks the spot where in 1431 Joan of Arc was burnt at the stake. Now the patron saint of France, she is remembered in the adjacent futuristic church, which dates from 1979. The superb 16th-century stained glass windows were retrieved from the St-Vincent church, which was destroyed in 1944.

The nearby market hall is used by farmers from the outlying rural areas to sell their cheese and also their bread, often baked in wood-fired ovens. In the autumn, freshly pressed cider in large glass bottles will be on sale too.

Musée Jeanne d'Arc

A row of ancient half-timbered buildings border the south side of the square. Sample the taste of Normandy in one of the traditional restaurants here and pay a quick visit to the **Musée Jeanne d'Arc** with its waxwork models. The birth-place of the great French dramatist, Pierre Corneille (1606–84), is now the ★ **Musée Corneille** (4 rue de la Pie) ❷. His study contains chairs, armchairs and other 17th-century furniture.

The ★ **Rue du Gros-Horloge**, now a pedestrian precinct, starts at the southeast corner of the Place du Vieux-Marché. This busy, cobbled street contains modern shops, most of which have been rebuilt since World War II, but they are in stark contrast to the many other medieval half-timbered buildings in the town centre.

The **★★ Gros Horloge** ❸ is a large clock which has become one of Rouen's principal tourist attractions. The golden clock-face which resembles a flaming sun was installed in the arch over the street in 1527. The adjoining **beffroi**, or bell-tower, once played an important part in a dispute between the people and the state. In 1382, when another tax increase was announced, a group of angry citizens organised a revolt by ringing both bells in the tower. King Charles VI's response was simply to demolish the upper part of the tower, thereby depriving the townsfolk of an important weapon.

Rue du Gros-Horloge and detail of the clock

Nowhere in the network of alleys and lanes is the medieval architecture quite so striking as on the **Place de la Cathédrale**. This extensive square is dominated by the impressive west facade of the **★★★ Cathédrale Notre-Dame** ❹, one of the finest examples of French Gothic. Started in the 12th century, it was not finished until 1530 and it contains many examples of the changing style of Gothic architecture. The eye is automatically drawn to the rose window at the centre of the west front and then the multitude of ornate figures. The 82-m (268-ft) **Tour St-Romain** on the left dates from the 12th century, while on the right the late Gothic **Tour de Beurre** with 56 bells was built between 1485 and 1507. The term 'butter tower' refers to a practice adopted during the Middle Ages. During Lent, wealthy citizens who did not wish to fast bought a dispensation. The amount that the church collected was known as 'butter money' and this money is said to have been used to build the tower. Topped by a cast-iron spire, the middle tower is the highest tower in the country (151m/495ft). All three portals are surrounded by statues and sculptures.

Cathédrale Notre-Dame

An almost mystical feel pervades the dark interior, often emphasised by a rich smell of incense, as the huge walls surrounding the 135-m (442-ft) long and 28-m (91-ft) high

Tomb of William Longsword

Escalier de la Librairie

Rue Malpalu

nave keep at bay the city's hustle and bustle. The choir and crypt are certainly the oldest parts of the building, which was constructed on the remains of a Roman temple. The ambulatory holds the recumbent figures of three famous Normans, each one having made his mark on the history of the region. In the first tomb rests Rollo, whose oath sealed the Treaty of Clair-sur-Epte in AD911. In the second tomb lies his son Guillaume Longue-Epée (William Longsword), who enlarged the duchy of Normandy to the Cotentin peninsula and around Avranches. The third tomb contains Richard I, the Lionheart, who died on 6 April, 1199 from blood poisoning after he was struck by an arrow in battle. The tombs of the cardinals of Amboise can be found in the Lady Chapel, where Georges I d'Amboise and II – uncle and nephew – are shown kneeling. This early Renaissance tomb, which was created between 1515 and 1525, is one of the finest sculptures in the cathedral.

Two portals lead off the transept. The richly ornamented **Portail de la Calende** in the southern arm portrays the martyrs and the baptism of Jesus. The **Portail des Libraires** (Booksellers' Doorway) at the north side is more striking with a sculpture of the Last Judgement in the tympanum. Before leaving the cathedral through this doorway, take a quick look at the finely carved **Escalier de la Librairie** (Booksellers' Staircase).

The late Gothic Flamboyant style can be found on many of the sacred buildings in the town, including the fine example of ★★ **St-Maclou ❺**. The most remarkable feature about this church is that it was built in late Gothic Flamboyant style between 1437 and 1517, a period when Renaissance style was already well established. On the west front of this church, small when compared to the cathedral, stands a five-part porch with two carved Italian-style portals. On the northwest corner of the church, the figure of the naked boy is much photographed.

Rue Malpalu and **Rue Damiette** near St-Maclou give visitors the best impression of what the town centre would have looked like in the Middle Ages. The fine town houses were built between the 15th and 18th centuries. The best half-timbered houses in Rouen are said to be in ★ **Rue Martainville**, which runs along the northern side of the church. The wrought-iron lanterns and shop signs above timbers, many of which are cracked and bowed with age, help to create an authentic atmosphere. An entrance by 184-186 Rue Martainville leads to ★★ **Aître de St-Maclou ❻**, a rectangular inner courtyard. During the plagues of the 16th century this courtyard was used as a mortuary for the victims. Between 1630 and 1636, about 20 percent of Rouen's population perished from the Black Death. The carvings on the two-storey gallery, now used by students from the **Ecole des Beaux-Arts** (Academy of Fine Art), display macabre motifs of skulls, crossbones and various gravediggers' tools.

Carved skull in the Aître de St-Maclou

The church of ★★ **St-Ouen** ❼ stands in the small park adjoining the Town Hall (**Hôtel de Ville**). An abbey is said to have stood here in the 4th century. The lawn nearby marks the place where Joan of Arc was sentenced to death. In front of the judges and onlookers, she begged for forgiveness, swearing 'I will do everything you ask.' The best view of this Gothic church is from the south or east side of the old monastery garden, as from this angle the neo-Gothic west facade, a 19th-century 'eyesore', remains hidden. The 82m (268ft) central tower has become a symbol of the region. Topped with a ducal coronet it is known today as 'the Crown of Normandy'.

With a total of five museums, **Place St-Godard**, named after the church of ★ **St-Godard** ❽, is regarded as Rouen's cultural centre. The ★★ **Musée des Beaux-Arts** ❾ is perhaps the best known (Thursday to Monday 10am-noon and 2-6pm, closed Tuesday and Wednesday morning). It mainly houses works by Norman artists. A part of the museum is dedicated to Théodore Géricault (1791–1824), who was born in Rouen and spent his childhood there. French Impressionism is also well represented since some celebrated painters such as Claude Monet, Auguste Renoir and Alfred Sisley lived and worked in the region. The **Musée de la Céramique** ❿ is also interesting. By 1550, the production of quality pottery was making an important contribution to Rouen's prosperity and, around 1644, a design involving blue decorative work on a white background was adopted in the local factories. The museum documents the growth of Rouen's pottery industry.

Musée des Beaux-Arts

The **Tour Jeanne d'Arc** ⓫ in Rue du Donjon holds reminders of Rouen's darker hours. Joan of Arc was imprisoned in this former keep. It is said that she was tortured here on 9 May 1431.

The ★★ **Palais de Justice** ⓬ in Place Maréchal-Foch on the other hand represents a time of grandeur and wealth. Work started on this splendid building at the end of the 15th century under the direction of the cathedral architect Roulland le Roux. During the reign of François I, it housed the parliament of Normandy. Badly damaged during World War II, it has been fully restored. During the work an 800-year-old house with some Hebrew inscription was discovered– proof that this was once the Jewish quarter of the town.

Palais de Justice

While in Rouen, visitors should ask in the Syndicat d'Initiative for information on sightseeing tours to the monasteries in the Seine Valley (*see page 22*). The tourist office will also have details of boat trips around the port.

BRITAIN

Paris

FRANCE

A family outing

Route 2

Route des Abbayes:
Rouen – Le Havre (110km/68 miles)

The Seine makes its way to the Atlantic coast alongside chalk cliffs, wooded hillsides and country villages. In pre-Christian times the river was an important artery and it remains so. The Romans settled in farmsteads along its banks and founded important towns such as Juliobona, modern Lillebonne *(see page 24)*. With the advent of Christianity, monks also started to build their monasteries close to the river and in the centuries that followed these contributed greatly to the economic prosperity and cultural richness of the region. The modern Route des Abbayes runs more or less parallel to the river and although many of the abbeys are in a poor state, their splendour bears witness to a distinguished era.

The railway line from Rouen to Le Havre and Fécamp passes through Yvetot, 10km (6 miles) north of Caudebec-en-Caux *(see page 24)*. Buses between Rouen and Le Havre pass through Caudebec-en-Caux, as well as Boscherville, Jumièges, St-Wandrille, Villequier and Bolbec.

Sights

Just beyond the outskirts of Rouen, the Route des Abbayes passes through the Forêt de Roumare, before the ★ **Abbaye St-Georges-de-Boscherville** (daily except Tuesday, 1 November to 31 March) in the small village of St-Martin-de-Boscherville. Archaeologists have uncovered evidence that the site had previously been used as a heathen temple, but it was in the middle of the 11th century that Raoul de Tancarville, William the Conqueror's chamberlain, decided to build a monastery here and from 1114 it was run by Benedictine monks. The abbey church was completed in 1125 and represents one of the purest examples of Romanesque architecture. The columns which supported the three arches on the west front are badly mutilated, but the level of craftsmanship visible on the statue columns is unique to Normandy.

Among orchards and meadows lies one of the province's finest monuments, the ★★ **Abbaye de Jumièges** (daily 1 April to 15 June and 15 September to 31 October, 9am–noon, 2–5pm; mid-June to mid-September, 9am–6.30pm; winter months 10am–noon and 2–4pm). The huge west front of the former **Notre-Dame** abbey church is relatively well preserved. Built between 1040 and 1067 it was consecrated by William the Conqueror, but in the 12th and 13th centuries it underwent a number of alterations which reflected the contemporary architectural trends still visible in the shape of the imposing twin towers.

Abbaye de Jumièges

St Philibert, who lived around 654, is said to be the founder of the monastery. Plundered by the Vikings in 841, it was abandoned until 940 and over the next 70 years, the whole complex was rebuilt to its original dimensions. Furthermore, the abbey succeeded in advancing its economic and political influence in the region. As a visible proof of its increasing power, the abbey church was extended by the addition of two new naves and the **Eglise St-Pierre** was also enlarged. During the monastery's heyday, over 1,000 monks and 1,500 lay brethren lived in the complex which also owned extensive estates in the vicinity. The two Jumièges churches are linked by the pre-Romanesque **Passage Charles VI**.

Tower detail, Jumièges

23

Before the Hundred Years' War, indeed even before the beginning of the Wars of Religion in 1562, the decline of the abbey had started and it was not until the first half of the last century that historians started to assess the cultural and political impact of Jumièges. The government took charge of the ruined site in 1947.

The foundation stone for the **Abbaye Notre-Dame-de-Fontennelle** in **Wandrille-Rançon** (pop. 1,500) was laid even earlier than that of Jumièges. Around AD629 Count Wandrille decided to renounce his position at the court of King Dagobert. He later returned to the Fontanelle Valley and founded the ★ **St-Wandrille Abbey** which was to flourish until the Wars of Religion. It fell into disuse during the Revolution but in 1931 Benedictine monks returned. Guided tours (Monday to Saturday 3–4pm, Sunday 11.30am) include the inner courtyard which is entered from the **Porte de Jarente**, built in the 18th century by the bishop of Orléans. Apart from a transept and the cloister gallery, very little of the once fine Gothic abbey remains.

St-Wandrille Abbey

Caudebec-en-Caux (pop. 2,500) on the right bank of the Seine is the ideal place to stop for a short break. Of architectural interest is the late Gothic church of ★ **Notre-Dame** with its tower in the form of a stone tiara. In its shadow every Saturday, farmers and traders exercise their 600-year right to sell their produce in the **Place du Marché**. Much of the town was destroyed by fire in 1940, but the 13th-century Maison des Templiers survived and is now used as a museum.

Victor Hugo caricature and museum exhibit

Victor Hugo is responsible for putting **Villequier** (pop. 900) on the tourist trail. The estate of the Vacquerie family lies on the banks of the Seine and the son married Hugo's daughter, Léopoldine. During one of their many visits, a boat trip on the Seine ended in tragedy when their boat overturned and they both drowned. For the author the death of his daughter was a terrible blow and it became a recurring theme in his subsequent writing. The **Musée Victor-Hugo** is now installed in the Vacqueries' house and contains paintings, photos, drawings and other memorabilia. The tombs of Hugo's wife and members of the Vacquerie family can be seen in the church cemetery.

Lillebonne (pop. 10,000) was an important inland harbour for the Romans and William the Conqueror, recognising its strategic position, built a castle here, but only the 34-m (111-ft) round tower has survived. Nearby the **Musée des Arts et Traditions Populaires** (7 Rue Victor Hugo) houses many 18th- and 19th-century exhibits of historical interest. The museum (or the café in the Hôtel de Ville) can also provide the key to Lillebonne's best known sight, a ★ **Roman amphitheatre**, dating from the early years of the Roman occupation.

Château Filières, with its gleaming white facade of Caen stone, lies to the west of Bolbec near the village of **Gommerville**. Only the left wing of the original 16th-century structure remains. The rest was restored in the 18th century and is now furnished with antiques.

Musée du Prieuré

The **Musée du Prieuré** is to be found in **Harfleur** on the eastern edge of Le Havre and was used in the Middle Ages as a hospital for sick seamen. It now documents various aspects of local history. A half-timbered first floor has been added to the huge stone-built ground floor.

The **Prieuré de Graville**, also on the eastern side of Le Havre, is the last stop on the Route des Abbayes. Situated in rue Elysée-Reclus, the pillars in the nave of the chapel are part of the original Romanesque priory. The former monastery building now houses the **Musée du Prieuré de Graville**, with some fascinating examples of folk art, including statues in wood, stone and ivory. There is also an interesting collection of over 200 model houses, displaying in miniature a wide range of Norman architectural styles.

Route 3

Le Havre: Boulevard Albert I

Le Havre: The Norman phoenix

No town in Normandy suffered during World War II as
much as Le Havre. Apart from one or two exceptions,
the town centre had to be almost completely rebuilt after 1945 and Le Havre rose phoenix-like from the ashes
to acquire a new face and a new identity.

25

St Joseph's church

Direct trains link Le Havre to Paris via Rouen. Buses serve
Fécamp via Etretat and Honfleur or Caen via Pont-
Audemer.

History

1945 was not the first time that Le Havre evolved from
a town planner's drawing board. In 1517, François I
(1515–49) ordered the construction of a port to replace
Harfleur which was silting up. At the beginning of the
Wars of Religion the devoutly Protestant town passed to
the English after the Treaty of Hampton Court, but within
barely a year it was returned to France. After the government of Henri IV made attempts to modernise the port
facilities, it was left to the governor of Le Havre, Cardinal Richelieu, to complete the expansion. Jean Baptiste
Colbert, Louis XIV's minister of finance, culture and the
navy, was responsible not only for enlarging France's colo-
nial empire but also for developing overseas trade from
Le Havre, especially with the East Indies. Disputes with
England led to a bombardment in February 1694 and further attacks in July 1759 caused considerable damage.
However, economic prosperity returned later that century
with the independence of the American colonies in 1776,
as European trade with the New World shifted from English ports to French ports. Later, Le Havre lost its impor-

Contemplating the past

tant role as a naval base to Cherbourg, but by the middle of the 19th century the town's population of 58,000 was profiting greatly from transatlantic passenger transport and trade.

During World War I Le Havre was an important supply base for the Allied troops stationed in northern France and the Belgian government in exile sought refuge there. After the war, luxury passenger ships sailed from Le Havre to New York and the French Caribbean islands, and the town once again returned to prominence as a major transatlantic passenger terminal.

During World War II, however, Allied bombing brought destruction on a massive scale. 80,000 inhabitants lost their homes, 10,000 buildings were destroyed and as very little of the old town remained, almost total reconstruction started in 1946 under the direction of the French architect Auguste Perret.

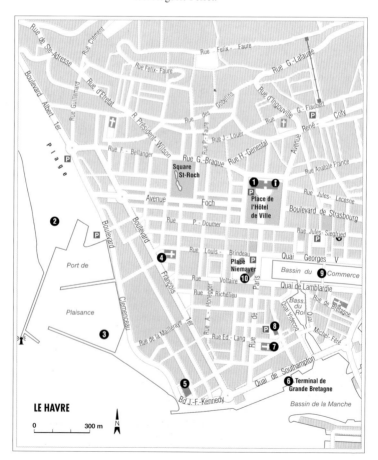

LE HAVRE

0   300 m   N

Sights

At the heart of the new town lies the **Place de l'Hôtel de Ville ❶**. Geometrical designs characterise this huge square, one of the largest in Europe. The plain **Hôtel de Ville** houses the city's administrative offices, as well as the **Office de Tourisme**.

Villa Maritime, Boulevard Albert I

Neglected by the local people for many years, Le Havre's **beach ❷** has undergone a facelift. The section of coast which runs parallel to **Boulevard Albert I** has been converted into a leisure area with a stream winding its way through the middle. Sports facilities, snack bars, restaurants and shops line the new promenade which is proving popular with the local people and also visitors.

Similarly, the municipal marina or **Port de Plaisance ❸** has become a favourite destination for a stroll on summer evenings. Overlooking the marina stands the plain concrete tower of **Eglise St-Joseph ❹**. Topped by an octagonal bell tower (109m/357ft), this 1950s church designed by Auguste Perret stands out on the city skyline. The bare walls of this striking monument are broken up by colourful, glass tiles which allow sufficient diffused daylight to enter the interior.

Eglise St-Joseph, interior

Only a few yards from the marina is the **Musée des Beaux-Arts André Malraux ❺**. (Daily except Sunday, 10am–noon and 2–6pm.) Another modern construction of glass, aluminium and steel, it was built in 1961 and has since become an important cultural centre. In front of the museum is a sculpture by HG Adam which dates from the same year. This huge concrete structure is known locally as the 'Eye', enhancing the centre's reputation as an top-class art museum – a reputation which now extends throughout France and beyond.

Most of the exhibits were formerly displayed in a museum which was destroyed in the last war. They represent a cross-section of European art from the last 300 years with many works by French, Flemish and Dutch painters. However, artists who painted in Normandy, such as Eugène Boudin, Emile Othon Friesz, Raoul Dufy, Claude Monet, Camille Pissarro, Georges Braque and Jean Dubuffet are given prominence.

Notre-Dame detail

Terminal de Grande-Bretagne ❻ is the destination for ferries arriving from England and is situated only a few yards from the town centre. The harbour attracts considerable interest from locals and visitors alike. On summer days the quayside is invariably congested with sightseers.

Those in search of peace and quiet, however, are more likely to find it in the **Cathédrale Notre-Dame ❼**. Completion was delayed by the Wars of Religion in the second half of the 16th century. The west front was finished in 1630 and the building then survived until World War II when it was badly damaged in bombing raids. The church

Bassin du Roi
Quartier St-François

The Passerelle

organ with beautifully carved wooden sections dates from 1637. It was not spared by the bombs either, but has been restored; *le Grand Orgue* was finally reinstalled in 1980.

A building nearby which suffered a similar fate is the **Musée d'Histoire Naturelle ❽**. The original museum was housed in Le Havre's Palais de Justice,which had to be completely rebuilt. Apart from the architectural loss many fine ornithological, mineralogical and zoological exhibits could not be replaced.

Just east of the museum lie the **Bassin du Roi** and the **Bassin du Commerce**, two inner docks which are linked to the outer harbour. These two docks form two sides of Le Havre's oldest district, the **Quartier St-François**. A glance at the map will show that it is almost an island, linked to the rest of the town with bridges. Formerly the site of the fish market, it too has yielded to recent modernisation. The **Musée de l'Ancien Havre** (1 rue Jérôme-Bellarmato) houses maps, plans and models which show clearly how Le Havre looked in the 19th century. The **Musée Maritime et Portuaire** (Centre Culturel Maritime, Hangar 22, quai de Norvège) is not just for amateur sailors with an interest in boats and boatbuilding, but for anyone interested in an era when dockworkers unloaded sacks of coffee from Brazil, cotton from India and spices from the Far East.

Looking like a concrete archer's bow supported by steel cables, the **Passerelle ❾**, a footbridge, crosses the Bassin du Commerce. It serves as both a short cut for pedestrians into the town centre and a viewpoint over the central **Place Niemeyer**. Here stands the principal symbol of Le Havre's rebirth, the ultramodern **Maison de la Culture du Havre ❿**. Opened in 1982, it was designed by the celebrated Brazilian architect Oscar Niemeyer. The complex consists of two asymmetrical buildings. The larger one houses a theatre, cinema and exhibition centre and is known to locals as *le Grand Volcan* (the big volcano), although it has been compared to the cooling tower of a nuclear power station or an upturned yoghurt pot. *Le Petit Volcan* is on a smaller scale and facilities here include an auditorium and conference rooms.

The sea still provides Le Havre with its prosperity. It is France's premier container port. The **Ecluse François I**, a huge lock 401m (1,315ft) long, 67m (219ft) wide and 24m (78ft) deep is one of the biggest locks in the world and can 'raise' vessels of up to 250,000 tons.

In the suburb of Graville, a little further out of the town centre, lies the **Abbaye de Graville** (Rue de l'Abbaye), where the Romanesque church of Ste-Honorine, one of the oldest sacred buildings in the Le Havre area, can be seen (*see page 24*).

Route 4

The Alabaster Coast:
Le Havre – Le Tréport (150km/93 miles)

The most spectacular section of the whole Normandy coast is the **Côte d'Albâtre** or Alabaster Coast. It forms the shore-line between Le Havre and Le Tréport in the Seine-Maritime *département*. The full force of winter storm waves thundering against the steep chalk plateau has created towering precipices and bizarre rock formations against a background of alabaster-white cliffs. Most settlements have developed at the river mouths – just a handful of houses or little towns. Interposed between the sea and the foot of the cliffs runs a long strip of coarse, shingle beaches bordered by mussel-clad rocks and tiny tidal pools littered with driftwood and seaweed, while at the cliff top a cool wind blows across the open meadows where seagulls perform their graceful aerobatics.

This route runs parallel to the English Channel, but the first 20km (12 miles) follow a northeastern course inland through gently undulating farmland. Etretat can be reached by bus from either Le Havre or Dieppe. Le Tréport (*see page 33*) is the rail terminus of the Atlantic coast line for Paris–Gare du Nord via Aumale and Eu.

29

Sights
Cap d'Antifer has become a paradise for windsurfers ever since the deep-sea harbour was constructed to accommodate supertankers unable to enter Le Havre.

★★ **Etretat** (pop. 1,500), hemmed in between steep cliffs, has for a long time enjoyed a reputation as an up-market holiday resort. Out of season, life in Etretat fol-

Etretat

Beauty on the beach

lows a steady pace, but the breathtaking scenery attracts thousands of visitors during summer and the surge of traffic often brings the town centre to a halt at weekends.

Sights in Etretat include the **Promenade** with views in both directions along the coast. Thursday is market day in Etretat and the medieval **market hall** in **Place du Maréchal Foch** is, like the one in Dives-sur-Mer, constructed from coarsely-hewn beams. Souvenir shops and boutiques now monopolise the space.

The market hall

The six bays with Romanesque decorations and the crossing lantern may draw some visitors to the church of **Notre-Dame** in Avenue Nungesser et Coli, but it is the stunning natural scenery that attracts most people and there are three walks to choose from.

At low tide a stroll from the western end of the promenade leads down across the steep shingle beach to a huge cave. While the bizarre rock formations look so fascinating, they are only accessible at low-water and seaweed and eelgrass can create a dangerously slippery surface. The adjoining oyster beds were laid before the French Revolution. A 60-m (200-ft) ladder leads up to a gallery with access to the ★★ **Falaise d'Aval** with an incomparable view along the stony beach and beyond.

The second walk follows the same direction but runs high above the steep bank along the clifftop.

For the third walk head east from the harbour up to the ★ **Falaise d'Amont**, on which stands the church of Notre-Dame-de-la-Garde with its splendid panoramic view over the town and coastline. A memorial and a small museum commemorate the achievements of the pioneering French aviators Charles Nungesser and François Coli who lost their lives attempting to cross the Atlantic in 1927.

Boules at Falaise d'Amont

The coast road to Fécamp passes through **Bénouville**, where walkers can park their cars and make their way through well-cropped meadows to the coast some 1.5km (1 mile) away. Steps lead down to the strangely weathered beach at **Valleuse du Curé**. Take care after wet weather as the steps can be slippery.

Vaucottes and **Yport** are small seaside resorts with shingle beaches. The latter with its colourfully painted boats presents a picturesque sight. Carthaginians may even have settled here, but certainly this region and **Fécamp** (pop. 20,800) were inhabited well before recorded time. Celts founded settlements on the cliffs before the area came under Roman influence. A monastery was established in the 7th century and pilgrims came to a shrine where drops of Christ's blood were kept. According to legend, persecuted Christians concealed the blood in the trunk of a fig tree and then cast it into the sea to be washed ashore at Fécamp.

Picturesque Yport

The monastery was plundered and destroyed by the Vikings but the Duke of Normandy, Richard I ordered it to be rebuilt and consecrated under the name St Trinité. In 1003, Richard II, the then Duke of Normandy, requested the reformer Guillaume de Volpiano to take over the monastery, which soon became a cultural and spiritual focal point within the duchy.

Fécamp monastery

The church of ★★ **St Trinité** with its 64-m (210-ft) crossing tower has undergone many changes since the days of Richard I, but the Romanesque building impresses mainly by its dimensions. Measuring 128m (420ft) in length, it is certainly the biggest in France. The lantern tower rises in a sweep above the crossing. The Precious Blood relic is kept in a marble tabernacle created by the Italian sculptor Viscardo in 1507. The church is the last resting-place for Abbot Volpiano (fourth chapel) and the Normandy dukes Richard I and II (baptismal chapel).

Apart from the church itself, another of the monastic community's legacies is a yellowish liqueur which brother Bernardo Vincelli first distilled in 1510. Full-scale production of the monks' distillation was later taken over by Alexandre Le Grand who built a factory and named it the ★ **Palais Bénédictine**. It is situated in rue Alexandre Le Grand and the architecture displays a clever blend of Gothic, Renaissance, Baroque and Rococo styles. Guides will explain the various stages of the production process. The adjoining museum houses a collection of medieval art, including paintings, wood and ivory carvings and furniture. (Daily January to mid-March and mid-November to end of December, 10.30am-3.30pm, mid-March to mid-November 9.30–11.30am and 2–5.30pm.)

Notre-Dame-du-Salut

There can be scarcely anywhere else on the coast road where the view along the cliffs is as striking as at the village of **Senneville**. The panorama near the chapel of **Notre-Dame-du-Salut** provides a superb view worthy of any calendar over the precipice and along the cliffs. On a clear day the view along the winding coastline extends as far as Etretat. Narrow valleys, like carved notches on the edge of a table, have cut their way through to the sea to create space for coastal settlements such as **Les Grandes Dalles** and **Les Petites Dalles** where there is just about enough space to turn a car round. More room is available in **Veullettes-sur-Mer**, located at the mouth of the river Durdent. The main source of employment here is no longer the land or the sea, but the nearby Paluel nuclear power station.

Les Grandes Dalles

St-Valéry-en-Caux (pop. 5,000) has been a popular centre for sailors for many years and the amateur mariners can be seen at the Friday market stocking up on provisions for the next leg of their voyage. Inland, set in parkland

Original furnishings in Château de Cany

Les Galets

Varengeville-sur-Mer

on the banks of the Durdent, lies **Château de Cany** (1 July to 1 September, daily except Friday 10am–noon and 3–6pm). The special charm of this building in magnificent Louis XIII style (1610–43) lies in the combination of bright stone and reddish-brown bricks and also in the fact that it is surrounded by a moat. The interior with its Flemish tapestries and original furnishings is also well worth a closer look.

Veules-les-Roses (pop. 800) is referred to by the local tourist office as a 'mini-Venice' and this may overstate the description a little, but it is situated at exactly the spot where the river Veules flows into the sea. Above the town, a weir stems the flow of the narrow watercourse to create a watercress jungle. Secluded footpaths follow an arm of the Veules along lines of pretty back gardens.

If now is the time for a bite to eat, then the **Les Galets** restaurant is worth seeking out (tel: 35 97 61 33, fax: 35 57 06 23). Do not leave without sampling the chef's speciality, a perfect lobster omelette.

Rather like Bénouville, to get to the stony beach in **Sotteville-sur-Mer**, it is necessary to descend 230 steps. Between the weirdly-shaped rocks, enthusiasts can extend their knowledge of sea fauna and flora or collect mussels and starfish.

Varengeville-sur-Mer (pop. 1,000) is only a small village but has more to offer the visitor than many of the other resorts and fishing villages along this section of the coast. Although it may only be viewed from the outside, the ★ **Manoir d'Ango** (March to November 10am–6pm, October to February weekends and holidays only) is a splendid example of a Renaissance manor-house. It was built by Italian craftsmen in the 16th century for the shipbuilder and shipowner Jean Ango. Much of the building material was specially imported from Italy. In the inner courtyard stands France's largest and most famous dove-cote. The brick and stone facing are arranged in an intricate geometric pattern.

In the nearby 10-ha (25-acre) ★ **Parc Floral Le Bois des Moutiers** (daily from Easter to All Saints' Day, 10am–noon and 2–4pm), Atlas cedars and oaks, colourful magnolia, camellias, azaleas and rhododendron thrive in the silicon-rich soil.

Parc Floral Le Bois des Moutiers

The view from the St-Valéry Romanesque church high above the cliffs is worth the climb and in the graveyard, the resting-places of three artists can be found: the painter Georges Braque (1882–1963), the writer Georges de Porto-Riche (1894–1930) and the composer Albert Rousel (1869–1937).

Pourville at the mouth of the river Scie is the last village before Dieppe (*see page 34*), but as a favourite summer retreat for many Parisians, it is sometimes referred to as the '21st Arrondissement'. It may be that they are drawn to the resort in the same way that the impressionist painters Auguste Renoir and Claude Monet were at the turn of the century.

The modest resort of **Puys** lies to the northeast of Dieppe and like Pourville was also a meeting-place for artists. Alexandre Dumas, author of *The Count of Monte Christo* and *The Three Musketeers*, died here in the home of his eponymous son (1824–95), a famous painter. Visitors to their home included the composer Claude Debussy who spent two summers with the Dumases.

Berneval-le-Grand

Berneval-le-Grand can also claim to have an artistic past. The clear light was an inspiration for the paintings of Auguste Renoir and the English writer Oscar Wilde sought refuge here after he had spent two years in prison for homosexuality.

The Alabaster Coast ends at the border with Picardy which is marked by the river Bresle. It flows into the sea at **Le Tréport** (pop. 6,300) which lies to the east of the river mouth. The neighbouring town of Mer-les-Bains is strictly speaking no longer in Normandy, but there is a fine view of Le Tréport's fishing port and the town's narrow lanes from in front of the station. The church of St-Jacques dominates Le Tréport's promenade and busy harbour. It is of late Gothic construction and possesses a fine *pietà* as well as some interesting votive plaques. High above the rooftops at the end of a long flight of steps stands the ★ **Calvaire des Terrasses**, an excellent panorama on the edge of the chalk cliff. Below, buffeted by the winds off the English Channel, the seagulls swoop noisily over the fishermen's cottages.

Le Tréport

Most visitors, however, are attracted to the beach at the foot of the towering cliffs, although the little town also boasts some excellent fish restaurants.

Route 5

Café life in the city centre

On the waterfront

★★ Dieppe: the starting point for French explorers

Visitors to the busy fishing and passenger port of Dieppe with its 40,000 inhabitants may well be unaware that, centuries ago, intrepid mariners set forth from this town to the then unexplored corners of the world. Men such as Jean Cousin, Thomas Aubert, Pierre Le Moyne d'Iberville and the Parmentier brothers said farewell to their families and explored as far afield as the island of Sumatra, the mouth of the Amazon, the St Laurence River and the Mississippi Delta. Seafaring in Dieppe has changed considerably since those days with modern roll-on roll-off cross-channel ferries now bringing thousands of British holiday-makers and day-trippers right into the heart of the town. How the opening of the Channel Tunnel will affect trade remains to be seen.

There is a direct rail link from Dieppe to Paris via Rouen. The CNA company runs bus services east to Le Tréport and west to Fécamp. A bus service from St-Valéry-en-Caux to Rouen connects with a service to Dieppe.

History

It is no accident that the word 'Dieppe' resembles the English word 'deep'. Early mariners identified the inshore waters and river mouth nearby to be both deep and safe and the banks soon developed into a thriving port. Dieppe played an important part in sustaining William the Conqueror in power after the Battle of Hastings in 1066 and enjoyed great prosperity up to the 17th century. The town also owes a considerable debt to Jean Ango II (1480–1551). His ships sailed the world and brought riches back to their home port and he later became an adviser to François I. The Florentine Giovanni di Verrazano served under Ango and later went on to discover the site of what was to become New York.

The Wars of Religion and plague epidemics put a brake on further prosperity and a bombardment by the English navy in 1694 resulted in the almost total destruction of the town and its wooden houses. It took many years for Dieppe to recover, but the fishing industry and the growth of lace-making in the 18th century helped to reverse the town's declining fortunes. 1824, however, saw the start of a new era. The fashion for sea-bathing brought wealthy visitors to the town and by 1860 as many as 3,000 English holidaymakers were coming to the resort each year.

In August 1942, a force of 6,000, mainly Canadian, troops failed in their attempt to recapture Dieppe from the Germans. Over 1,000 soldiers lost their lives.

The sights

The ★ **panorama ❶** on the edge of the cliff above the old castle is easy to reach if approaching Dieppe from the south or west. From this position above the town, it is clear that Dieppe – nestling between steep cliffs at a point where several small rivers, including the Eaulne, Béthune, Varenne, Arques and Scié join the sea – is indeed the perfect place for a port.

As early as the 17th century, Dieppe fishermen became suppliers of fresh seafood to the French court. Scallops from Dieppe are still regarded as a delicacy among discriminating gourmets.

The ★ **Vieux Château ❷** or old castle dominates the western end of the town (June to September, daily 10am–noon and 2–4pm; October to May closed Sunday). The huge 15th-century structure with defensive towers at each corner was built by the master fortress builder Vauban and has been altered on many occasions. Initially it was the home of the town's governor, but was later converted into barracks. In 1923 the municipal museum (**Musée du Château**) took over the site and with the fine collection of ivory carvings it earned a reputation far be-

The Vieux Château is famous for its ivory

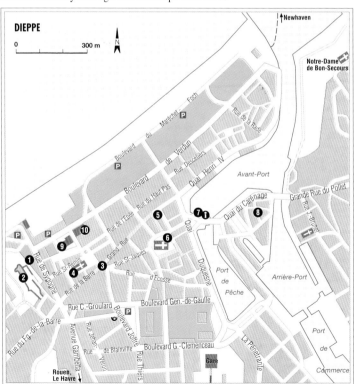

yond the town itself. As early as the 14th century, Dieppe mariners had been returning from the West African coast with the 'white gold'. Skilled artisans carved both religious and everyday objects out of this precious material and Dieppe became the European centre of the ivory trade until well into the 19th century.

Place du Puits-Salé

In the centre of **Place du Puits-Salé 3** in front of the Café des Tribunaux stands a well and, as the name suggests, it was a source of salt water. A few yards away stands **St-Rémy** church **4**. The Wars of Religion delayed its completion, but it was between 1552 and 1645 that most of the work was undertaken. It has suffered damage on a number of occasions and has always been restored, but little of the original remains, apart from the Gothic choir and the Louis XIII-style facade.

The busy, traffic-free **Grande Rue** – a continuation of Quai Henri IV – links the Place du Puits-Salé with the port. Traditional *charcuteries* and long-established butchers' and bakers' shops stand alongside T-shirt shops and fashionable boutiques to create a lively thoroughfare. A monument in the **Place Nationale 5** commemorates Abraham Duquesne (1610–88), who commanded the French fleet under Louis XIV.

Charcuterie

The church of ★ **St-Jacques 6** has the appearance of a guide book on ecclesiastical architecture. The oldest, Gothic sections are the remains of an earlier building which was largely destroyed by Phillip II's soldiers around 1195. While much of the exterior is Gothic in style, parts of the interior, mainly the choir, Lady Chapel and sacristy, are in the Flamboyant or Renaissance style. A substantial amount of the work in the church was financed by the Ango family. Yet another style is in evidence in the 42-m (138-ft) tower, which closely resembles the Tudor style of many church towers to be found on the other side of the English Channel.

Salut! – Port de Pêche locals

Pont Jean Ango 7 separates the **Avant Port** (ferry port) from the **Port de Pêche** (fishing port) and links the commercial heart of Dieppe with **Le Pollet 8**, the fishermen's quarter with narrow alleys and small cottages.

High above this eastern suburb stands the ★ **Chapelle Notre-Dame-de-Bonsecours**, with a fine view over the rooftops to the chalk cliffs in the west. Votive tablets inside provide an insight into the fears and anxieties of fishing families.

Washing in Le Pollet

Most of Dieppe's cheaper restaurants are to be found on the Quai Henri IV along the northern side of the ferry harbour, while the open spaces on the seafront are bordered by **Boulevard du Maréchal Foch** close to the beach and the **Boulevard de Verdun** which runs in front of the hotels, the remains of the town's fortifications, the **Porte des Tourelles 9** and the **casino 10**.

Route 6

The rustic charm of Pays de Bray

The Pays de Bray:
Le Tréport – Gisors (120km/74 miles)

If cider and apple brandy are synonymous with the Calvados region (*see page 49*), then the Pays de Bray means cheese. Best known among them is the cheese from Neuchâtel. Fresh spring water flows into rivers and streams, lush broad-leaf forests flourish in the valleys and hollows and spa towns such as Forges-les-Eaux prosper from the mineral-rich water in which Louis XII, Queen Anna of Austria and Cardinal Richelieu relaxed.

Cheeses for sale

Away from the little towns and villages, the green meadows and pasture land of the Bray country have changed little from the days when kings, queens and distinguished French statesmen came here to take the waters. It is safe to assume that savouring the famous local cheeses was just as important to these pillars of church and state as the health cures and casino.

For many years the Pays de Bray, snuggling between the plains of Picardy, the Pays de Caux and Normandie-Vexin, was known as Paris's 'pretty farmyard' and any Frenchman who orders a *café au lait* on Boulevard St-Michel in the heart of the capital will know for certain that the milk flowed from the udder of a Normandy cow with black patches around each eye – as if the farmer had fitted a pair of sunglasses.

Forges-les-Eaux (*see page 39*) is at an important rail junction where the line from Paris to Dieppe crosses the line from Rouen to Amiens. CNA buses run between Rouen, Forges-les-Eaux and Aumale. If making for Gisors (*see page 40*), the D921 which runs due south of the town is a more interesting route than the D915.

*William and Matilda
on their wedding day*

Sights

Only 3km (2 miles) inland from Le Tréport in the Bresle valley lies the town of ★ **Eu** (pop. 8,000). It was here that Rollo, the first duke of Normandy, died in 932. And when William the Conqueror married his cousin Matilda of Flanders in 1050, the couple chose Eu as the setting for the great event. The inscription on the roughly-hewn rock in **Place Guillaume-le-Conquérant** is a reminder of the wedding, while the castle in which the festivities were held stood only a few yards away.

That site is now occupied by a Renaissance **château** which was begun in the second half of the 16th century. It was a favourite residence for French king Louis-Philippe, who entertained Queen Victoria and Prince Albert here in 1843 and again in 1845. Some of the rooms are given over to the **Musée Louis-Philippe**, which houses a mixture of old masters and contemporary furniture. The **Chapelle du Collège** was built by Catherine of Cleves in 1620. Her mausoleum is on one side of the altar. On the other is that of her husband, Henri Guise, who was murdered on the orders of Henry III.

Notre-Dame-et-St-Laurent

Opposite the castle stands the church of ★ **Notre-Dame-et-St-Laurent**. Dating originally from the 12th and 13th centuries, it was fully restored in the 19th century. The triple-naved interior with the main nave divided up with arcades, triforium and loft serves as a perfect example of early Gothic. The ambulatory consists of a number of chapels each decorated with sculptures. The superstructure of each chapel is for structural reasons secured by a network of arched buttresses. Behind the altar lies the tomb of the archbishop of Dublin, Lawrence O'Toole who died in Eu in 1181. The crypt is guarded by stone carvings of the dukes of Artois.

Glass-making has a long tradition in the Bresle Valley and in **Blangy-sur-Bresle**, the **Verrerie Waltersperger** in Avenue de la Gare offer guided tours of the factory. Visits are arranged through the Syndicat d'Initiative in Blangy (tel: 35 93 52 48). Glass-blowers can be watched at work by the furnace. Some products are produced using traditional methods, but a wide range of the company's glassware is produced using automated equipment. The Waltersperger factory and others in the region specialise in small perfume and spirit bottles made from coloured crystal glass. They come in many different shapes, sizes and colours and make unusual but attractive souvenirs. Other glass factories in the area concentrate on making test tubes for the pharmaceutical industry.

Northwest of Neufchâtel-en-Bray in the Béthune valley lies the ★ **Château de Mesnières-en-Bray** (1 April to 1 November Saturday and Sunday 2–6pm), which resembles some of the châteaux in the Loire Valley. With

Château de Mesnières-en-Bray

a pointed round tower on either side of the entrance steps, this castle, which was built by Louis XV, appears to be a combination of a fortification and country house. The interior of this magnificent building, which is now used as a boarding school, is the outstanding architectural masterpiece of the Bray region. Its salient features include the **Salle des Cartes** with its 17th-century works of art, which are painted not on canvas but on wood, and the 16th- and 19th-century chapels. The older of the two is decorated with some delightfully carved wooden statues representing Christ, John the Baptist and the four apostles, Matthew, Mark, Luke and John.

Neufchâtel-en-Bray (pop. 5,400) was badly damaged in 1940 and only a few original buildings remain. The oldest parts of the church of **Notre-Dame** date from the 12th century and the 400-year-old nave and splendid stained glass windows make a visit worthwhile. A manor house contains the **Musée d'Art Régional**, where tools of cheese-, clog- and saddle- makers can be seen.

Neufchâtel is known throughout France for a delicious cheese which is marketed under the same name and sold in a variety of shapes. Sadly many small-scale farmers using 'traditional' methods have seen cheese production fall into the hands of large dairies, such as those in Neufchâtel, which use state-of-the-art technology in the cheese-making process.

A few farms continue to use traditional methods to make the local cheese. Two of them are just a short distance from Neufchâtel and are happy to open their doors to visitors. A telephone call in advance is appreciated. M. Brianchon, Ferme des Fontaines, Nesle-Hodeng (on the D135) tel: 35 93 08 68 (March to November); M Auvre, Mesnil-Mauger (on the D120), tel: 35 90 41 22.

Forges-les-Eaux (pop. 3,800) was once a famous spa town and attracted many celebrated guests. Today the little town is a quiet but refined oasis in an area otherwise dedicated to farming. Iron deposits were discovered by the Romans who used them to make weapons, but at the beginning of the 16th century the town began to prosper when the healing qualities of the mineral springs were acknowledged and bathing in the waters became a fashionable pastime for the wealthy. Louis XII, Anne of Austria and Cardinal Richelieu were convinced of the water's powers. Forge-les-Eaux's reputation as a spa town thus became well established and, centuries later, visitors still come to 'take the waters'. The spa region of the town is confined to the area along the banks of the Andelle, which widens out into a lake to the north and south of the Avenue des Sources. The **Grand Casino** is another major attraction and not just for spa guests. Voltaire is said to have tried his luck at the original casino.

Back to the soil in Neufchâtel-en-Bray

39

A sign of fine cheese

The Grand Casino

Route 7

In the footsteps of Richard the Lionheart through Normandie-Vexin:
Gisors – Giverney – Rouen (120km/75 miles)

The region known as Normandie-Vexin lies to the southeast and only just inside Normandy proper and yet in the 10th century it was at the heart of the duchy. Later on, Richard the Lionheart sought to protect the eastern and southeastern flanks against French intrusion and the solid fortifications he created bear witness to this time.

Two's company

Vernon is on the Paris to Rouen railway line. Bus services connect Vernon, Evreux, Gaillon, Les Andelys and Gisors.

Sights

★ **Gisors** (pop. 9,000) is only a small town, yet as the capital of the Normandie-Vexin region, it can look back to a stirring past. The most important factor in the town's development was its strategic position, on a hill above the Epte Valley on the southeastern edge of Normandy and 900 years ago this was considered an ideal location for a fortress with which to secure the French/Norman border. The castle or ★★ **Château Fort** which overlooks the town and dates from 1097 owes its existence to the then king of England and duke of Normandy, William II, William the Conqueror's son.

Gisors' bold Château Fort

Despite the alterations of later years, the castle at Gisors is a fine example of medieval castle construction and this is due partly to the fact that it has been well-preserved and partly to the bold architectural style. The keep and public gardens are located inside a huge ring wall, which was built so solidly that visitors can still safely climb the steps to the 20-m (65-ft) viewing platform.

Among the houses below, the two towers of the church of **St-Gervais-et-St-Protais** are clearly visible. The ceiling and interior were badly damaged during World War II and it has taken many years to restore them to their original condition. Similarly, when the church was started in the 12th century, it took 400 years to complete – hence the juxtaposition of Gothic and Renaissance elements. Despite the range of architectural styles, the church creates a unified, harmonious impression.

Only 15km (9 miles) southwest of Gisors lies **St-Clair-sur-Epte**, the cradle of Normandy. It was here in AD911 that the French king Charles le Simple and the Viking leader Rollo agreed the treaty which laid the foundation for an independent duchy. At that time Rollo controlled the larger part of Norman territory and the treaty officially ceded that land to Rollo. The Vikings, for their part, agreed to stop their violent campaigns and Rollo agreed to adopt Christian beliefs. The church where this treaty was agreed by a solemn oath still exists and on the 1,000th anniversary of the agreement, the village fathers installed a window showing Rollo kneeling at the feet of the king.

For many lovers of art there is no village in France more important than **Giverny**. The impressionist painter Claude Monet lived there between 1883 and 1926 and, soon after his death, the house was turned into the **Musée Claude-Monet** (from the beginning of April to the end of October, daily 10am–6pm). It draws visitors from all over the world. The best time to appreciate the peace and quiet the painter enjoyed is early in the morning before the queues form outside the pink-washed house. The rooms are painted in different pastel shades with light blue, for example, in the reading room and cream in the bedroom where the painter died. The kitchen wall is covered with Delft tiles.

Monet's house at Giverny

The interior has different pastel shades

Most of his attention, however, was devoted to the **garden** where nothing was left to chance. He chose the various flowers according to their precise time of flowering and thanks to his meticulous planning was able to fulfil his dream of a summer garden with at least some flowers constantly in bloom. The painter spent hours in his garden with brush and palette in hand creating those world famous paintings which now hang in the top galleries of Normandy, Paris and elsewhere.

41

Giverny is actually only a suburb of **Vernon** (pop. 23,500). For many Parisians this pleasant town is the gateway to Normandy. The French king, Phillip II, must have viewed the town in the same light when he seized it from the Normans in 1204. During the Hundred Years' War Vernon returned to English rule for about 30 years, before it finally was returned to the French.

Claude Monet Garden

Stained glass in Notre-Dame

Vieux Moulin

42

In the centre of Vernon stands the church of ★ **Notre-Dame** which was begun in the 12th century but work continued into the 16th century. A superb rose window with elements of Flamboyant style dominates the west front.

The oldest house in the town, known as *Au Temps Jadis* (In Days Gone By), will inevitably attract attention. This medieval half-timbered structure is currently used to accommodate the tourist information office. The **Hôtel de Ville** or Town Hall was completed at the end of the last century. A walk through the old town's narrow alleys with their half-timbered houses is to get close to life in the Middle Ages. The **Musée Alphonse-Georges-Poulain** (12 rue du Pont) displays artefacts of archaeological and regional interest as well as a small collection of paintings, including some by Claude Monet.

Near the Pont Clemenceau in Vernonnet, a district of Vernon, stands one of Normandy's most frequently photographed places, the **Vieux Moulin**. This 16th-century mill has been lovingly restored. A few yards further on stands the **Château des Tourelles**. This partially ruined castle was constructed in the early Middle Ages to protect a bridge which once crossed the river Seine at this point.

The small town of **Gaillon** (pop. 6,300) on the left bank of the Seine is noted for the **Château de Gaillon** which represents a milestone in castle architecture. It suffered badly during the Hundred Years' War and was rebuilt in 1453, but the most significant event in the castle's lifetime is attributed to Cardinal Georges d'Amboise who gave orders for the castle to be converted into a summer residence in Italian Renaissance style. The castle can only be seen from outside and yet it is worth stopping to admire it, even if only for the view from the castle forecourt over the tiled roofs to **Les Andelys** in the Seine Valley. Situated high above the river valley, ★★ **Château Gaillard** (from mid-March to mid-November, daily 9am–noon and 2–6pm) has played an important role in the history of Normandy. It was built in the 12th century as part of a defensive ring intended to thwart the aggressive intentions of the French crown. Once Phillip II had captured Gisors in 1196, Richard I ordered the construction of this castle as a replacement and it was completed within a year. It remained in Norman hands for only a few years. On 6 March 1204, this proud fortress fell to Phillip's men, thereby opening up the way through to Rouen. Only parts of the curtain wall and fortress remain.

Richard the Lionheart's Château Gaillard

The Normandie-Vexin route leaves the Seine Valley and heads northeast towards the 10,000 ha (25,000 acre) **Forêt de Lyons**. In earlier times, the woods would have echoed to the sound of hunting horns as the dukes of Normandy

followed closely on the heels of deer and wild boar. Now oaks and beech with particularly beautiful leaf variegations in autumn attract walkers and gourmets in search of mushrooms. In 1138, in the heart of the forest, Henri I Beauclerc, one of William the Conqueror's sons, founded a Cistercian abbey. However, only ruins remain of the 90-m (295-ft) long and 40-m (130-ft) wide church of the **Abbaye de Mortemer**. But the crumbling, ivy-strewn walls, windows and ledges still give a clear impression of the dimensions of this former monastery.

Lyons-la-Forêt (pop. 700) is a small, picturesque centre for walkers, who will find a wide selection of footpaths to choose from. In the centre of the village, the marketplace is dominated by an 18th-century market hall with a fine timber roof.

The château at **Vascœuil** attracts considerable interest from tourists. It was built between the 14th and 16th centuries and was for 30 years the home of the French historian, Jules Michelet (1798–1874). A museum within the château is dedicated to him.

The small village of **Ry**, however, attracts much greater interest. Students of French literature will recall the fictitious settlement of Yonville in Gustave Flaubert's *Madame Bovary* as it is said that the village was based closely on Ry. A bust of the Norman writer stands in front of the post-office.

The ★ **Château de Martainville** in **Martainville** has a certain fairy-tale quality about it and, as the last stop on this route, the castle with its pointed towers, dormer windows and brick chimneys is definitely worth a quick look. The building also accommodates the **Musée Départementale des Traditions et Arts Normands** (daily 10am–12.30pm and 1.30–6pm; 2–5pm in winter). On display are late medieval furniture and artefacts from rural life. Rouen is 16km (10 miles) to the west.

18th-century market hall, Lyons-la-Forêt

43

Abbaye de Mortemer

The château at Vascœuil

Château de Martainville

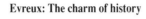

Route 8

*Evreux cathedral
and the River Iton*

Evreux: The charm of history

Ducks rest beneath tall trees on the river banks, a small bridge crosses the water in a gentle arc and *impatiens* carpet the embankment. Add a picture-frame and a signature to this tableau and it would then be easy to believe that with a few swift brushstrokes Claude Monet had painted the scene.

Evreux is on the Paris St Lazare–Cherbourg railway line. The town is linked by bus to the towns of Vernon, Rouen, Brionne, Conches and Nonancourt.

History

Not everything in Evreux is quite so romantic as river scene by the River Iton. Centuries of history have left their

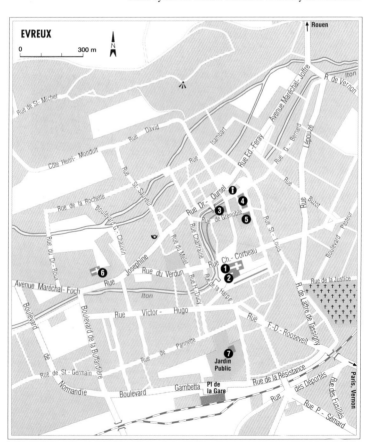

mark on this town of about 50,000 inhabitants. Tales of war and destruction in Evreux go back to the 5th century when Vandals sacked the town, which had been founded by the Romans on the site of a pre-Christian Celtic settlement. In the 9th century the Vikings razed the town and in 1119 the English king Henry I burnt down the wooden town centre. When John, brother of Richard I (the Lionheart) seized Normandy, he ordered the massacre of the entire French garrison and their commanding officers. In reprisal, Philip II decreed that the town be burnt to the ground. During the Hundred Years' War, the cycle of devastation and reconstruction continued and in World War II, many old buildings were destroyed by bombs.

Sights

The **Cathédrale Notre-Dame** ❶ with its Renaissance-style west facade of niches, ledges and pillars and dissimilar towers is best viewed from the Promenade du Miroir d'Eau. On windless days this image is reflected in the river – a popular theme for photographers.

Cathédrale Notre-Dame, exterior and detail

A passage links the cathedral with the former **bishopric** or **Palais Episcopal** ❷. It stands on the site of fortifications erected by the Romans in the 3rd century and remains can be seen inside the Palais in the **Musée d' Evreux**. Another exhibit on view in the museum is a figure of Jupiter dating from the 1st century BC.

The central business quarter of Evreux has department stores, and many small shops line **Rue du Dr Oursel**. The **Beffroi** ❸ nearby, dating from the 15th century, overlooks the town. This delightful tower rises to a height of 44m (144ft) and in fact consists of two separate towers, each with its own spire. In the higher of the two towers hangs a bell which is almost 600 years old and weighs two tons. It and two smaller bells chime on the hour. In late afternoon the belfry's shadow extends as far as the **Hôtel de Ville** ❹ and the neighbouring **Théâtre Municipal** ❺.

The Beffroi

Saint-Taurin ❻, where the first bishop of Evreux is said to be buried, dates from the 14th century but a closer inspection will reveal sections of the building which date from two to four centuries earlier. One important treasure which the church guards is St Taurin's Shrine. This masterpiece of French craftsmanship recounts events from the life of the saint. This gleaming reliquary is in the form of a 1.2-m (4-ft) high and 1-m (3-ft) wide miniature chapel and bears testimony to the craftsmanship of French gold and silversmiths during the 13th century.

The perfectly formed cloister in the **Ancien Couvent des Capucins** ❼ dates from the 17th century and serves as evidence of the Capuchin monks' skills. It is not difficult to imagine the brethren picking herbs in the beautiful garden until called to prayer by the bell.

Honfleur harbour

Route 9

The Calvados Coast:
Côte de Grâce and Côte Fleurie (32km/20 miles)

The French hosts and their international guests sip aperitifs in the beach cafés, strollers and sun-worshippers parade up and down the wooden platform, while on the restaurant terraces, the secluded world of rural Normandy merges with sophisticated and fashionable metropolitan life to create a world-renowned resort.

The Calvados Coast between the mouths of the Risle in the east and the Orne in the west is a collection of superlatives: magnificent beaches, picturesque harbours and exclusive seaside resorts. For the stretch of coast between Honfleur and Cabourg, the descriptions Côte de Grâce (Coast of Grace) and Côte Fleurie (Floral Coast) can be applied with full justification.

Trains link Paris St-Lazare with Trouville/Deauville via Lisieux, continuing on to Dives-sur-Mer and Cabourg. Connections to Honfleur, Deauville and Caen. Cabourg is served by buses linking Caen and Le Havre via Honfleur. In Honfleur boat trips on the *Vedette Stephanie* depart from Quai des Passagers, tel: 31 89 91 49.

Sights

Eating outdoors at the Vieux Port

The harbour or ★★ **Vieux Port** at **Honfleur** (pop. 8,200) forms an inner courtyard surrounded like a castle wall by lines of narrow houses some with seven storeys. At the end of the 15th century, seafarers like Binot Paulmier de Gonneville and Jean Denis sailed off into the unknown on voyages of discovery and on 15 March 1603 Samuel de Champlain set sail from Honfleur in the *Bonne-Renommée*

to cross the Atlantic and five years later he founded the Canadian city of Quebec.

If the 16th and 17th centuries belonged to these mariners, then the 19th century was the artists' heyday. Eugène Boudin *(see page 82)* came from Honfleur and his paintings of the sky and the sea paved the way for the impressionists. Boudin rented a room from Mère Tantain in **Ferme Saint-Siméon** paying 40 francs a month including meals, and with a view from the window over the beautiful coastline, he indulged his passion for painting. Other painters such as Corot, Courbet, Harpignies, Isabey, Troyan and Diaz were also inspired by Normandy's clear light and worked in Honfleur. The **Musée Municipal Eugène-Boudin** in Place Erik-Satie evokes memories of Honfleur's artistic past (13 March to 30 September, daily 10am–noon and 2–6pm; 1 October to 12 March, Monday to Friday 2.30–5pm, Saturday and Sunday 10am–noon and 2.30–5pm; 1 November to 13 February closed Tuesday).

Ferme Saint Siméon

In the vicinity of the swing bridge, between the inner and outer harbour, stands the **Lieutenance** or Governor's House. Built during the 16th and 17th centuries it was formerly a part of the town's fortifications.

The wonderful wooden **church and belfry of ★ Ste-Cathérine** lies further towards the town centre. Built in 1468, this church contains two identical naves with timber roofs and wooden pillars. Once your eyes have adjusted to the gloom, many fine wooden carvings can be seen. Every Saturday a colourful market occupies the square in front of the church.

Ste-Cathérine

Above the town stands ★ **Le Calvaire** with the chapel of **Notre-Dame-de-Grâce**. This graceful 17th-century building is visited by pilgrims, mainly seafarers, every year. A little higher the Mont-Joli panorama affords excellent views over the rooftops and along the coast.

★ **Trouville-sur-Mer** (pop. 5,600) and Deauville sit on either side of the River Touques and the two towns vie with each for the holiday trade. Trouville is more popular with families than Deauville which attracts well-heeled, international jetsetters. Both resorts have wide, sandy beaches but in Trouville the casino, swimming pool, municipal **aquarium** and water therapy institute, close to the mouth of the river, also attract many visitors.

Dozing in Deauville

The Pont des Belges connects the two towns across the river. With a population of 5,000, **Deauville** has become one of France's top resorts and certainly the most exclusive holiday centre in Normandy. The main attractions are the Boulevard Cornuché with its white casino and the wooden plank promenade known as ★ **Les Planches** which runs alongside the swimming pool, ten-

Child's play

Dives-sur-Mer

The medieval market hall

nis courts, mini-golf course and pony club. In the summer, parasols and sunbeds in red and blue set off against the white sand create a *tricolore* effect. Deauville's reputation is due in no small way to the many cultural events such as film and music festivals which draw international names. Major sporting contests include the polo championships, horse-racing and sailing.

★ **Villers-sur-Mer** is situated on the zero line of longitude and a line on the promenade represents the spot. In the world of palaeontology, the town has a special significance as huge numbers of fossils have been found in the chalk cliffs known as the *Vaches Noires* (Black Cows).

The small coastal town of ★ **Houlgate** (pop. 1,700) lies on the east bank of the River Dives and is recognised as an exclusive seaside resort with some superb summer residences along the sea front. In Rue Henri-Dobert, *Columbia*, *Merrimac*, *Minnehaha* and *Tacoma*, four American Renaissance-style villas, are the most striking.

Just south of Houlgate the coast road heads inland towards **Dives-sur-Mer**, a small town with a population of about 6,000. It was here in 1066 that William the Conqueror assembled his fleet before setting sail for England. Above the **Notre-Dame-de-Dives** church portal, the names of the 475 men who accompanied the Duke of Normandy on his voyage across the English Channel are listed. The finest building in the central market square is the medieval **market hall** with its well-maintained timber roof. Every Saturday morning farmers and market traders, customers and onlookers pack the dimly-lit hall where the tables are laden with fresh vegetables, shiny apples, sausages and crusty bread.

Opposite the market hall stands another historic building, the **Lieutenance**, the former residence of the Lord of Falaise, which possesses a tall, restored facade. It is a shame that aromas of Norman cuisine no longer emanate from the windows of the medieval **Village Guillaume le Conquérant** inn. Instead, a range of undistinguished toys and souvenirs are on sale here.

★ **Cabourg** (pop. 3,400) owes much of its fame to the celebrated French writer Marcel Proust (1871–1922). At the beginning of the 1880s, he came to Cabourg in the hope of bringing some relief to his asthma. Only 20 years earlier, the town had been laid out in a geometrical, semi-circular pattern with all the main roads meeting at the square in front of the **Grand Hôtel**. Even in his later years, Proust made his way up to his writing desk in room 414 of the hotel. Cabourg has become a literary monument as a result of Proust's 13-volume masterpiece *A la Recherche du Temps Perdu* in which it features as the town of Balbec.

Route 10

Cider, Calvados and Camembert:
The Pays d'Auge (150km/93 miles)

There is no area of Normandy where it is harder to stay sober than the Pays d'Auge. But it is not alcoholic drinks which are the intoxicants, rather the rolling hills, secluded copses, green meadows, remote half-timbered villages and narrow country lanes which wind through the shady valleys and broad pastures like a roller coaster.

Lisieux (*see page 52*) is on the Paris St Lazare line to Caen and Cherbourg. A branch line links the town with the Côte Fleurie. Bus services link Lisieux with the nearby towns of Pont-l'Evêque, Honfleur, Livarot and Vimoutiers.

Sights

A foretaste of what lies ahead can be found in the village of **Cricqueville-en-Auge**, which lies just to the south of **Dives-sur-Mer**. Reddish-brown bricks alternate with light-coloured stones to give the castle facade the appearance of an outsized chess board. Better known is the village of ★ **Beuvron-en-Auge** (pop. 275). The houses look so immaculate. Perhaps the mayor himself takes a tin of paint and a paintbrush every evening to touch up the beams. Beuvron is one of the *villages préservés* where the villagers care about the upkeep of their old homes. In this case the loving attention extends to maintaining window-boxes of glorious, colourful geraniums – creating an image much appreciated by the visitors and their cameras. Every farmhouse by the roadside sells home-made cheese, fresh butter, calvados and preserves made *à l'ancienne*.

Cricqueville-en-Auge

49

Beuvron-en-Auge

If the displays of home-made produce have whetted the appetite, then the place to go is a Ferme Auberge such as the Ferme-Auberge du Laizon in **Cleville** (signposted from Beuvron), tel: 31 223 64 67. Reservation essential. Even the aperitif of icing sugar, calvados, crème fraîche and a pinch of nutmeg is a revelation, if certainly not low in calories. Choose a main course from rabbit *à la normande* or lamb cutlets which the proprietor grills in the dining room as chickens wander in and out through the open door in search of crumbs. And after a night-cap of well-fermented cider, a beautiful soft bed!

Crèvecoeur-en-Auge

Crèvecoeur-en-Auge (pop. 550) owes its place on the Pays d'Auge sightseeing route to the ★ **Château de Crèvecoeur** (1 May to 30 September, 10am–1pm and 2–7pm; mid-February to end of April and beginning of October to end of November, 11am–1pm, 2–6pm). The entrance hall is unusual with coloured stones in a che-

Manoir de Coupesarte

Oil prospecting in the Musée de la Recherche Pétrolière

Livarot Cheese is cone-shaped

querboard pattern typical of the region at the base of the round portal. It is the sort of place where a watchman might at any moment open one of the leaded windows on the upper floor and rudely demand to know who is seeking entry. In addition to the geometrical timber design and cone-shaped, weatherboarded towers at the flanks, there are a number of other buildings which deserve a closer look including the farmstead, barn and dovecote, although the main attraction is the fortress with the Schlumberger museum. The **Musée de la Recherche Pétrolière** is run by the Schlumberger Foundation, whose funds derive from two French industrialists and oil-prospectors.

Grandcamp-le-Château castle is in private hands and its owners shield themselves from prying visitors by a moat and wall, but it is possible to catch a glimpse of the grounds from the small bridge which crosses a pretty stream by the main entrance.

The rustic charm of the ★ **Manoir de Coupesarte** will entrance visitors, who are welcome to view the manor from outside but are really only tolerated in the grounds. It stands in the middle of a man-made lake and is surrounded by trees whose branches overhang the water.

Livarot (pop. 2,500) is not noted for any historical sights, but its cone-shaped cheese has put the little town on the map. Locally-produced cheeses and many others are on sale at the busy Thursday market. A bigger market takes place every Monday in **St-Pierre-sur-Dives**, 16km (10 miles) to the east. The town is a flourishing centre for arable and livestock farmers and the size of the **Halle aux Grains** or Corn Exchange stands as a monument to its founders, the monks from the ★ **Abbaye de St-Pierre-sur-Dives**, who as early as the 13th century recognised the potential of the surrounding farmland. The abbey church was built in the 12th century on the foundations of an earlier Romanesque church. A new section was added in subsequent centuries: the crossing tower in the 13th century, the west front and north tower in the 14th century and the upper part of the nave in the 15th century. This grand abbey is regarded by many as one of the finest sacred buildings in the whole of Normandy.

A detour to **Vimoutiers** (pop. 5,000), south of Livarot, follows the pretty Vie Valley. In the town's market square stands a monument to Marie Harel, a farmer's wife who is credited with bringing to the attention of a grateful world Normandy's most valuable export, Camembert cheese. The history of the cheese and the story of how it is produced is documented in the **Musée du Camembert** (10 avenue de Gaulle). The building is a reproduction of a cheese-making plant and it has on display many colourful Camembert labels.

Monument to Marie Harel

Musée du Camembert

A few minutes to the southwest by car lies **Camembert** itself, a name known as widely throughout the world as the Eiffel Tower, though the village has had to hand over the production of this famous soft cheese to Vimoutiers. The **Ferme de la Héronnière** is a working farm open to visitors, where the traditional methods of cheese production are still followed (daily except Sunday). A phone call in advance is appreciated, tel: 33 39 08 08.

51

The moated ★ **Château St-Germain-de-Livet** on the banks of the Touques is one of the most popular sights in the Auge Region. (1 October to 31 March, 10am–noon and 2–5pm; 1 April to 30 September, 10am–noon and 2–7pm; Wednesday in summer until 11pm. Guided tours available upon booking, tel: 31 62 07 70.)

The popular Château St-Germain-de-Livet

At the entrance to this remarkably beautiful house with chequerboard walls of natural stone and clinker bricks stand two slim cone-topped towers. The roof of the left-hand tower is, for some reason, slightly bigger and it sits on the substructure like an oversized hat. On the right-hand side, the chequered front facade stops abruptly by the entrance to make space for a half-timbered structure with a saddleback roof. It is precisely this asymmetrical pattern which lends character to the building which has been owned by the town of Lisieux since 1957.

The external promise of St-Germain-de-Livet is almost matched by the interior. To pass from the entrance hall with chimney and Renaissance frescoes up to the upper storey where the original 16th-century tiles cover the floor and valuable Louis XV furniture is displayed gives some insight into the lifestyle of aristocratic Normans. The Delacroix Room does not house paintings by the eponymous artist, but a collection of his furniture, although he never actually resided in the castle.

The graceful interior

*Basilique Ste-Thérèse
and monks*

*Half-timber in
Rue Henry-Chéron*

Lisieux (pop. 26,500) is the biggest town in the Pays d'Auge and the commercial, industrial and religious centre. Established as a bishopric as early as the 5th century the town and its Carmelite monastery where Ste Thérèse was once a nun have been a place of pilgrimage for decades. All the year round, coach-loads of pilgrims from France and beyond make their *pèlerinage* to Lisieux where the town's shopkeepers who sell plastic saints have been making a comfortable living from the believers' faith and devotion for many years.

The primary destination for the pilgrims is the huge **Basilique Ste-Thérèse**, dedicated to the nun Thérèse Martin. She was born in Alençon in 1873 and the family moved to Lisieux four years later, living in a house known as Les Buissonnets. As a nine-year-old girl she tried to enter a convent, but was regarded as too young. Five years later, on a pilgrimage to Rome, she was granted a dispensation by the pope and on 9 August 1888 as a 15-year-old novice was admitted to the Carmelite convent in Lisieux. Sadly, her extraordinarily pious life in the convent lasted only nine years. She died in 1897 of tuberculosis, but just prior to her death she wrote the story of her short-lived spiritual pilgrimage, *L'Histoire d'une Âme* (The Story of a Soul). She was canonised in 1925.

The huge cathedral was consecrated in her honour in 1954. The architects have, however, not heeded Ste-Thérèse's message of humility and moderation, apparently believing that sheer size is the true measure of all that matters in this life. The basilica, made from white stone, consists of a 95-m (311-ft) high dome, a nave 30-m (98-ft) wide and 37-m (121-ft) high and a number of smaller towers. The result is that the whole building resembles a combination of St Peter's Cathedral in Rome and a Turkish mosque. The crypt is also of vast dimensions with space for thousands of worshippers. **Les Buissonnets** (Ste-Thérèse's home) in Boulevard Herbert-Fournet is also much visited by pilgrims. It consists of the dining room and bedroom where the young Thérèse lived with her father, brothers and sisters before entering the convent.

Old Lisieux was badly damaged by fire during the battles of 1944 and so the former *capitale du pan de bois* (half-timbered capital) is only visible in a few places, such as Rue Henry-Chéron, Rue du Docteur-Degrenne and Rue Docteur-Lesigne, where the old houses have been rebuilt.

Evidence that Lisieux was formerly an attractive town with many historic buildings can be found in **Musée du Vieux-Lisieux** (38 boulevard Pasteur) where watercolours, engravings and old photographs are on display. Some exhibits such as traditional furniture, Norman pottery and traditional Pays d'Auge folk art were saved from the pre-war museum and are housed here.

The church of **St-Pierre** in the town centre stands on a site of historical significance. It was in the original church in 1152 that the Plantagenet king of England, Henry II married Eleonore of Aquitaine, whose marriage to the French king Louis VII had been annulled. This marriage had momentous significance as thereafter large areas of French soil passed to the English crown. Two hundred years later, the consequences of this marriage sparked off the Hundred Years' War in which the English king, Edward III, laid claim to the French throne.

St-Pierre

The modern Eglise St-Pierre was started in the 12th century, but subsequently underwent many changes. As the first Gothic church in France, it has a special place in French architectural history. Bishop Pierre Cauchon who condemned Joan of Arc to death is buried in the Lady Chapel. The old **episcopal palace** which stands next to the church was built in the 17th and 18th centuries and now functions as the *Palais de Justice*. The painted ceiling and the walls lined with gilded Cordoba leather in the **Chambre Dorée** (Golden Room) are well worth a quick look.

The episcopal palace

Pont-l'Evêque (pop. 4,000) is, after Camembert and Livarot, the third small town in the Pays d'Auge noted for its cheese. It lies just a few miles from the Côte Fleurie. This square, soft, creamy cheese has been produced in Pont-l'Evêque since at least the 17th century. Another local speciality is the tasty, pink-fleshed trout which do not need to have their scales removed. The River Touques is one of the best places in France to fish this species.

The 'Père Malgloire' distillery in the Route de Trouville produces calvados using the traditional methods. It takes several years for the otherwise colourless liquid to mature and develop the much valued amber tinge. 'Père Malgloire' store about 2,000 oak casks in their cellars. As the **Musée du Calvados et des Métiers Anciens** (daily 10am–12.30pm, 2.30–6.30pm) adjoins the distillery, it is possible to sample a drop or two of the prized liquid.

Musée du Calvados

On the way from Pont-l'Evêque to the Côte Fleurie, on the side of the hill near the village of **Bonneville**, stands the **Château de Guillaume le Conquérant**, or at least what the ravages of time have left behind. It was from this castle in 1066 that William looked out over the English Channel and decided to launch his attack on England. The old walls have crumbled and now only ruins and a tower remain, but there is still a fine view to enjoy.

The last stop of this tour is at **Touques** with its rows of old houses beneath bowed rooftops. This once important town now stands in the shadow of Deauville. It is said that the murdered Thomas Becket visited the church of **St-Thomas** shortly before he met his violent death and hence it is consecrated in his name.

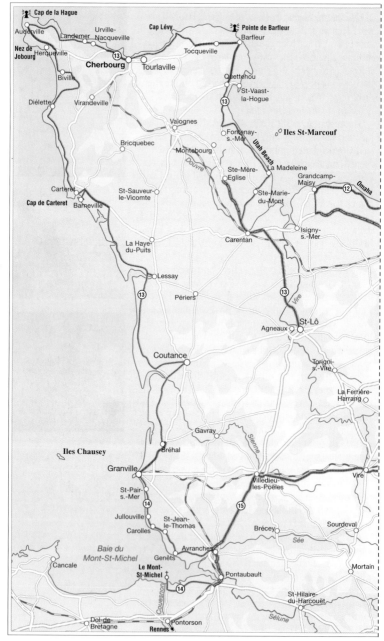

54

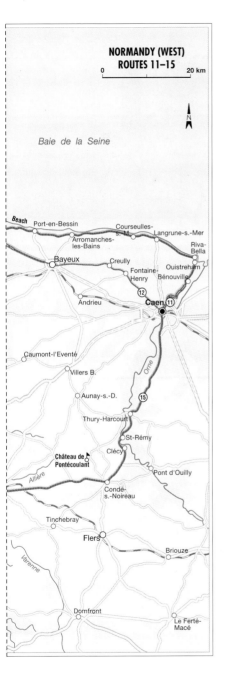

NORMANDY (WEST)
ROUTES 11–15

0   20 km

N

Baie de la Seine

Beach
Port-en-Bessin
Courseulles-s.-M.
Langrune-s.-Mer
Arromanches-les-Bains
Riva-Bella
Bayeux
Creully
Ouistreham
Fontaine-Henry
Bénouville
(12)
Andrieu
Caen (11)

Caumont-l'Eventé

Villers B.

Orne

Aunay-s.-D.
(15)

Thury-Harcourt

St-Rémy

Clécy

Château de Pontécoulant
Pont d'Ouilly

Allière

Condé-s.-Noireau

Tinchebray

Flers

Briouze

Varenne

Domfront
Le Ferté-Macé

55

Abbaye aux Hommes
Preceding page: detail from the
Bayeux Tapestry

Route 11

★★ Caen: a roman jewel with a smooth, modern finish

*Stained glass window
in the Abbaye aux Hommes*

Caen has survived military campaigns, wars, rivalry and revolutions and many scars still remain, but to step from the brightness of a summer evening into the peaceful shadows of the Abbaye aux Hommes with its vaulting, arcades, pillars, buttresses, roofs and pointed towers, it is easy to forget the conflicts of recent years and imagine a tranquil scene 900 years ago when the abbey church had just been consecrated.

Caen was once the town where William the Conqueror lived, but its importance now is as a city of the arts, a showpiece of Romanesque style, one of the best towns for shopping in Normandy and, with a population of 183,000, the administrative centre of Basse Normandie. A good market is held in the Place St-Sauveur every Friday.

Direct rail connection from Paris to Cherbourg. The 'Bus Verts' link Caen with the Ouistreham terminal, where ferries arrive from Portsmouth, and then continue on to Courseulles via Luc-sur-Mer. A good local bus service operates within Caen and the city is also linked to the bus network which serves Calvados and beyond.

Friendly locals

History

During Gallo-Roman times this settlement in a marshy region on the banks of the Orne was known as Cadomus. It only came to prominence in the 11th century when William the Conqueror chose it as his official residence and built a castle there. When Pope Nicholas II raised the order of excommunication against William, who had married his cousin Matilda of Flanders without papal dis-

pensation, the couple founded two monasteries, the Abbaye aux Hommes and the Abbaye aux Dames – now regarded as the two finest examples of Romanesque architecture in Normandy.

In the next two centuries Caen attracted people from a variety of backgrounds and in 1204 the French occupied the town. However, it was captured by the English in both 1346 and 1417, before it was restored to the French in 1450. In 1432 a university was founded in the town.

A plague took its toll on the population in the 16th century and then the Wars of Religion brought a period of violence to the town, as Protestants and Catholics plundered each other's churches. The town also had to endure difficult times during the French Revolution when it became a refuge for anti-Revolutionary Girondistes as they sought to escape – vainly as it turned out – from the Montagnards' reign of terror.

Like many other Norman towns, Caen suffered badly during World War II, mainly during the two-month battle for the town after the Normandy landings in June 1944. In the years after the war almost the whole of the city centre had to be rebuilt.

57

Sights

On a hill in the centre of the city stands the **château ❶**. It was built by William the Conqueror in 1060 and in subsequent centuries, it underwent many changes. During the Revolution much of the fortress building was removed, but that was not the end of the citadel's place in history as it played an important strategic role during the battle for the city in World War II and by the end of the siege only a ruin remained.

The château by night

It was rebuilt after 1945 and new cultural centres occupied this prime site in the heart of the city. Two museums were opened and Caen became a focus for the arts. In the **Musée des Beaux Arts ❷** (daily except Tuesday, 10am–noon, 1.30-5pm; in summer, 1.30–6pm), the works of Veronese, Tintoretto, Rubens, Le Brun and Boucher and many other famous 17th-century French and Italian masters are on display. Special exhibitions bring together works by painters such as Monet and Courbet who were inspired by the Normandy landscape. The museum also possesses over 50,000 engravings as well as an unusual collection of Rouen faïences.

Musée des Beaux Arts

History rather than art is the theme of the **Musée de Normandie ❸**, which occupies the former governor's residence inside the citadel. Exhibits from the region's prehistory, early years, Gallo-Roman times and the Viking period are displayed here. Other artefacts which document the region's history include a variety of costumes, tools and furniture.

Musée de Normandie

The oldest parts of the **Chapelle St-Georges**  date from the 12th century, but the chapel itself was rebuilt in the 15th century.

Caen's city centre and business quarter lies beneath the **Porte sur la Ville** on the south side of the castle with the church of ★ **St-Pierre** ❺ directly in the foreground. There can be no doubt that this building is the late Gothic jewel of Normandy. A golden weathercock has topped the 78-m (255-ft) spire for many years, but like so many similar pieces of exposed metalwork its movement has rusted and it no longer turns.

Inside the church the apse beneath the stained glass windows is by far the most interesting feature. The delicate masonry resembles filigree lacework.

How the town houses of Caen would have looked before the war can be seen in the historic **Hôtel d'Escoville** ❻ in Rue St-Jean. The building, strongly influenced by the Renaissance style, was built by a wealthy businessman according to plans drawn up by an Italian architect. The tourist office is accommodated here. At 52 Rue St-Pierre, behind an ancient half-timbered facade with carved beams, the **Musée de la Poste et des Techniques**

Musée de la Poste

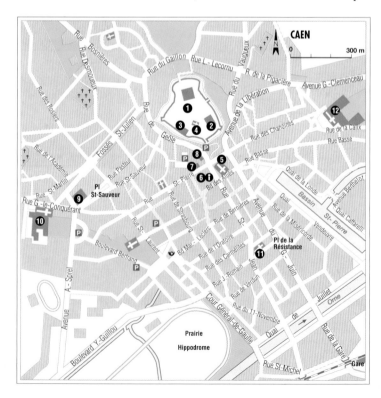

de Communication ❼ can be found. As well as exhibits from the days of stagecoaches and postilions, early communication systems such as the telegraph are displayed.

Another fine half-timbered building is the ★ **Hôtel des Quatrans** ❽ in Rue de Geôle (no. 31). This three-storey house with leaded glass panes was begun in the 14th century. The inner courtyard creates an authentic medieval atmosphere.

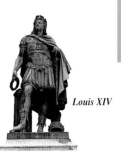

Louis XIV

In the middle of the small but charming **Place St-Sauveur** stands a monument to the Sun King, Louis XIV. The church of **St-Sauveur** with its combination of Gothic and Renaissance deserves a quick visit.

From the **Palais de Justice** ❾, there is a clear view of one of Caen's two main sights, the ★★ **Abbaye aux Hommes** ❿ with the abbey **church of St-Etienne** (Esplanade Jean-Marie Louvel; guided tours start on the hour between 9am and 5pm). It represents William's atonement and a gesture of reconciliation between himself and the pope, who had excommunicated the duke from the church after his marriage to Matilda of Flanders. In 1077 the abbey, unsurpassed for its austerity and severity, was consecrated. Ten years later William found his last resting-place here after a riding accident. His tomb is marked, but the grave was ransacked and his bones scattered. Lanfranc, the first abbot and later the archbishop of Canterbury, is generally credited with the design of the Romanesque west front. The Gothic apse with its four belfries was added in the 13th century, together with the two spires to the square towers. These were destroyed by Protestant troops in 1562 during the Wars of Religion, but were faithfully restored in the next century. In the 17th century, a new middle belfry was built to replace a 120-m (393-ft) tower which had collapsed. The monastery building is now used by the city administration as offices and was the work of Guillaume de la Tremblaye, architect to the Benedictine monks of St-Maur.

The abbey church of St-Etienne

To reach the Abbaye aux Dames, cross the city centre and shopping quarter, paying a brief visit to the church of **St-Jean** ⓫ on Place de la Résistance. It is a splendid example of late Gothic Flamboyant architecture. A landslide caused the tower to lean slightly.

St Jean: sculpture detail

The ★★ **Abbaye aux Dames** or Abbaye de la Trinité ⓬ (guided tours: Monday to Friday 2.30–4pm; Saturday also 10–11.15am) is the sister building to the Abbaye aux Hommes and lies in the east of the town by **Place de la Reine Mathilde**. It owes its existence to Queen Matilda and was built for the same reason as the men's abbey. In 1080, only three years after it was consecrated, its founder was buried in the centre of the Romanesque church. While the dimensions of the Abbaye aux Hommes seem so impressive when viewed from the outside, the

Abbaye aux Dames

Modern windows in La Trinité

women's abbey is of more modest proportions. The differences in the interior are equally striking. While St-Etienne remains largely true to its original design, the recent restoration of La Trinité has brightened the nave. Some modern features such as a new altar and red and blue windows in the Romanesque choir have changed the interior's character and there are divided opinions as to the final effect. Similar doubts arose after a 19th-century restoration was deemed to have upset the architectural harmony of the building. A black marble plaque in the choir identifies the grave of Queen Matilda, who died in 1083.

The convent buildings, which were designed in 1704 by Guillaume de la Tremblaye, survived until the French Revolution. Thereafter it was used as a warehouse but in the last century the abandoned section was converted into a hospital. It is now the seat of the regional council for Basse Normandie.

Outside the confines of the city, beyond the campus of the university founded by the Duke of Bedford in 1432, lies a memorial of more recent times, the **Musée pour la Paix** in Esplanade Eisenhower. Its subject is the history of the 20th century, with particular emphasis on the causes and events of World War II. All the latest technology is employed to convey facts and information about Normandy's darkest hours.

Visitors should note that on summer weekends the tourist office organises a three-hour guided tour of Caen. On Tuesday and Friday in July and August, evening tours lasting an hour and a half visit the best known sights. Reservations can be made in the tourist office.

Musée pour la Paix

Route 12

BRITAIN

Paris

FRANCE

Sandy beaches:
The Côte de Nacre and Le Bessin (160km/99 miles)

Time heals many wounds. In the very places where on 5 June 1944 under the cover of night the Allied forces landed to begin the invasion of France, local people join together with guests of every nationality to enjoying the sea and sandy beaches beneath steep cliff faces. There are still many places, however, where history intrudes. The remains of this huge military undertaking – war cemeteries, rusted tanks, memorials and the sections of the man-made harbour of Arromanches – can still be seen. Where once amphibious landing craft fought their way on to the beaches, now brightly painted fishing boats and expensive yachts bob up and down.

Arromanches Harbour

Memories of the war impinge on everyday life in so many ways. The inhabitants of Colleville, for example, have tagged 'Montgomery' on to the name of their village, so that the name of the commander of British ground forces on D-Day would never be forgotten. Less honourable, perhaps, are those who, 50 years or so later, seek to profit from the war by buying and selling medals and uniforms. Violence and war have certainly left their mark on this coastal region, but intellect and culture are in evidence just as much here as anywhere else in France. In the picturesque provincial town of Bayeux, which suffered little damage in 1944, the famous *Bayeux Tapestry* still draws countless tourists every year. They stand and stare in their tens of thousands stunned by this colourfully embroidered story book which depicts William the Conqueror's victory at the Battle of Hastings in 1066.

61

Happy to be back on dry land

Bayeux (*see page 63*) is on the railway line which links Paris, Caen and Cherbourg. A branch line connects Bayeux with St-Lô, Coutances, Pontorson and Mont St-Michel. A good bus service links Bayeux with the Côte de Nacre resorts and Caen.

Sights

The **Côte de Nacre** or the Pearl Coast is how this part of Normandy is often described. The name refers to the section between Ouistrehem/Riva-Bella and Grandcamp-Maisy. The hinterland is known as **Le Bessin**, a lush pastureland ideal for dairy herds. In between the two lie villages where one might expect to find tumbledown cowsheds rather than proud Renaissance castles such as Fontaine-Henry. This route starts and finishes in Caen and many will be able to complete it in a day, but a leisurely pace will prove more rewarding.

Port en Bessin

Pegasus Bridge,
symbol of liberation

Musée du Débarquement

Omaha Beach

Caen, the administrative centre for Basse Normandie (*see page 56*), lies about 15km (9 miles) from the coast but is linked to the sea by the Canal de Caen à la Mer. The main road follows its course towards the English Channel via **Bénouville**. Here the river Orne and the canal were spanned until 1993 by the historic **Pegasus Bridge**. This point was one of the Allied forces' first objectives and was taken by British parachutists. Although it stands at a busy bottleneck, it was not easy for the road-planners to dismantle this symbol of the liberation of France and replace it with a new structure.

The origins of **Ouistreham/Riva-Bella** (pop. 6,700) are not entirely clear. The fine beach at Riva-Bella obviously played its part in attracting visitors during the 19th century. A casino and the Institute for Thalassotherapy also helped to boost its popularity. In 1986 a new ferry crossing opened between here and Portsmouth, but whether it will be able to withstand the competition from the Channel Tunnel remains to be seen.

Probably the main destination for visitors to this region is **Arromanches-les-Bains** (pop. 500). Its coastal location and fine beaches are not the reason for the interest it arouses, but the part it played in the D-Day landings. 'Operation Mulberry', the construction of a man-made harbour in the bay off Arromanches, was one of the most ambitious schemes of World War II. Pontoons were towed over from the south coast of England and secured to the sea-bed. Once complete with a total of 33 jetties and 16km (10 miles) of floating 'roads', it enabled the Allies to supply the troops with 9,000 tons of material each day. By the end of August over 500,000 tons had been landed, but then other Channel ports became available and the temporary harbour was no longer needed. At low tide, sections of the harbour are still visible, but they are now covered with green seaweed and mussels. For a more detailed account of the events of those momentous days, visit the **Musée du Débarquement**, by the car park near the beach (daily 9am–6.30pm, Monday 10am–6.30pm).

Port-en-Bessin-Huppain (pop. 14,500) is a lively and popular resort. The harbour with brightly coloured yachts and motor boats creates a picturesque scene and is a favourite with amateur photographers. Bars and small restaurants overflow on to the pavement and on a fine day there is no better place to relax. For lunch, make your choice from the local *boulangerie* and *charcuterie* and then take the main road to the south of the village where there is a clean and shady picnic site which is equipped with tables (and toilets).

The Allied forces code-named the stretch of shoreline off Laurent, Colleville and Vierville-sur-Mer **Omaha Beach** and this turned out to be the scene of one of the landing's bloodiest battles with the American 1st Infantry Division bearing the brunt of the losses. The **American Military Cemetery** in **Colleville** was consecrated in 1956. While about 14,000 dead were repatriated to the United States, white marble crosses remember the 9,386 American soldiers who were buried here. Over 300 crosses mark the resting-places of unidentified soldiers. The memorial is laid out as a semi-circular colonnade with a loggia at each end. The 7-m (23-ft) high bronze figure symbolises American youth.

There is a tremendous view over Omaha Beach from a panorama which lies between the memorial and the coast. In one or two places, narrow lanes lead down to the beach which is ideal for swimming and sunbathing.

The American Cemetery

One of the fiercest battles for control of Omaha Beach took place at **Pointe du Hoc**, an exposed headland and a site of great strategic importance. It is one of the few places which still gives the impression of having been a battlefield – gun emplacements, destroyed bunkers, shell craters and bent metal litter the site. A great deal of blood was spilt here before it was finally captured.

Pointe du Hoc

Grandcamp-Maisy lies at the western end of the Côte de Nacre and at low tide on warm days when the sun warms the seaweed and the tiny sea creatures on the mudflats then the distinctive smell of the sea can pervade the air. The River Vire which flows into the Atlantic here has over the centuries brought alluvial sand down to the shore line creating the ideal conditions for oyster and mussel beds. City dwellers are often puzzled by the sight of tractors on the beach at low tide, but that is the time when the fishermen 'harvest their crop' and the low-lying walls surrounding the beds can be seen in the distance. Despite pessimistic predictions, the seafood business has become very profitable in recent years.

For the journey back to Caen from Grandcamp-Maisy, say farewell to the coast and head inland to the region known as Le Bessin. Near **La Cambe** on the RN13 stands a reminder that many German soldiers also lost their lives in the battle for the Normandy coast. Over 21,000 bodies lie buried in the German cemetery and a huge granite cross looks down from a hill over the graves.

★★ **Bayeux** (pop. 13,000) is the administrative centre of Le Bessin and offers history with a picturesque backdrop. On the banks of the River Aure, which flows through the heart of the town, two wooden waterwheels recall the days of corn mills and of carpenters who shaped the beams for the half-timbered facades in the narrow lanes, creating a medieval atmosphere. But the sight of tourists is also very much part of the day-to-day scene as the town possesses probably the best known of all Normandy's sights.

In the years which followed the Battle of Hastings, not only was a work of art of great beauty and skill created, but also a unique piece of historical evidence. The *Bayeux Tapestry* documents in precise detail the events leading up to the decisive battle and those that followed. The French call the tapestry ★★ **Tapisserie de la Reine Mathilde** and it is displayed in the **Centre Guillaume-le-Conquérant** in Rue de Nesmond, tel: 31 92 05 48 (daily, mid-March to mid-May, 9am–12.30pm, 2–6.30pm; mid-May to mid-September, 9am–7pm; mid-October to mid-March, 9.30am–12.30pm, 2–6pm).

The Bayeux Tapestry

Centre Guillaume-le-Conquérant

A presentation in an ante-room with sound and pictures help to set the scene and provide the historical context. The tapestry itself, however, is as well protected as the Crown Jewels. Bullet-proof glass keeps curious visitors at a respectable distance and dimmed lights create not only a mystical atmosphere but help to retain the colour of the embroidery.

The tapestry measures about 70m (230ft) long and half a metre (18 inches) wide and the story is told in a series of pictures sewn with coloured wool. It is tempting to draw comparisons with a comic strip, particularly when the faces and figures are studied closely. Helmeted horsemen with shields and swords look down at their spread-eagled opponents. But it is not only the battle, which is depicted in the tapestry. The conflict is presented in a wider context. The illustrations tell, for example, how King Harold on an earlier visit to Normandy renounced his claim to the English throne and how, in scene 17, he saved two Norman soldiers in St Michael's Bay. Animals, weapons, tools and erotic scenes fill the borders above and below the main pictures. Some symbols can also be identified and histo-

The Bayeux Tapestry

rians have used these to help reconstruct the precise details of the events leading up to the invasion.

The degree of detail is quite amazing. Altogether there are 58 scenes with descriptions in Latin and a total of 623 figures, 759 animals and 37 ships and buildings. The tapestry was probably unveiled on 14 July 1077 when the new Bayeux cathedral (*see below*) was consecrated. Who was responsible for the needlework is uncertain, but some evidence suggests that it was commissioned by Odon de Conteville, the then bishop of Bayeux, and finally completed in England. Within its 900-year history, it has only twice left Bayeux. In 1803 Napoleon had it displayed in the Louvre in Paris as part of a propaganda battle with the foe across the English Channel and during World War II the tapestry was hidden away in a variety of places. The loyalty of the inhabitants of Bayeux to 'their' tapestry has been amply repaid. In post-war decades the tapestry has brought to Bayeux not only millions of visitors but a degree of prosperity which would surely have delighted William.

Work started on the ★★ **Cathédrale Notre-Dame** in 1047 and lasted for 30 years until it was completed by Bishop Oddo and consecrated in the presence of William himself. However, further work continued in the ensuing centuries as repairs were needed and account had to be taken of new architectural styles. A new crossing tower was added in the 18th century and topped with a Baroque 'bonnet' but there were serious concerns about the additional weight it imposed on the substructure. In the 19th century the decision was made to pre-empt a possible collapse and the foundations and other load-bearing structures were reinforced and a new spire added.

65

Bayeux cathedral

The interior of the cathedral is an impressive sight. The main features of interest are the 14th-century side chapels with their magnificently decorated capitals and also the chancel which dates from the 13th century. Restoration work and alterations usually bring structural and financial problems, but also surprises – in the 15th century a Romanesque crypt which had been filled with rubble was discovered underneath the cathedral.

It is tempting to assume that the tapestry and the cathedral are all that Bayeux has to offer, but that would be to overlook the beauty and atmosphere of the medieval old town with some houses dating from the 14th century. The **Office du Tourisme** is based in one of the oldest houses, a huge three-storey half-timbered structure with a steep roof. Similar houses such as the **Maison du Bienvenue** can be found in Rue de la Jurisdiction. Rue de Quincangrogne, Rue des Ursulines and Rue du Général-de-Dais also contain some fine houses.

Office du Tourisme

For wet days there is a wide choice of museums. A 'combination' ticket from the Centre Guillaume-le-Conquérant includes admission to these museums as well. For those who wish to discover more about D-Day then the **Musée de la Bataille de Normandie 1944** in Boulevard Fabian-Ware will be of interest. The **Musée Baron-Gérard** in Place de la Liberté houses exhibits of Bayeux lace and porcelain collections. Bayeux was an important lace making centre between the 17th and 19th centuries and there is still a lace-making school in the town. In the Hôtel du Doyen in Rue Lambert-Leforestier the **Musée Diocésain d'Art Religieux** contains exhibits of religious art and historical documents. One room recreates the scene in which the 15-year-old St-Thérèse asks the Bishop of Bayeux for permission to enter a convent.

Deep in the Seulles Valley lies the unassuming village of **Creully**, not a place, one would have thought, for medieval castles. The castle here has a massive keep in typical 14th-century military-style architecture with battlements and fortified towers mixed with an ornate Renaissance-style round staircase with a domed roof on the side facing the town, and visitors may well be confused about the buildings precise function. The castle has, however, had many owners, including Jean-Baptiste Colbert (1619–83), one of Louis XIV's senior ministers who introduced much-needed but unpopular tax reforms. In mid-1944 the place was taken over by new owners, the BBC. Broadcasters arrived and established a radio station intended to keep British (and German) listeners informed about the progress of the invasion. During the summer months, classical music concerts are held within the walls.

Château Fontaine-Henry

Further east along the Seulles Valley lies another medieval building, one often seen on calendars and posters, **Château Fontaine-Henry**. For information about opening times, tel: 31 80 00 42. This castle is just as much a part of Normandy as apple blossom. The original building was badly damaged during the Hundred Years' War but was restored by the Harcourt family in the 15th and 16th centuries. The Renaissance influenced the new facade of the castle which, together with the steep saddleback and cone-shaped roofs, as tall as the three storeys beneath, create a striking impression.

Treat yourself at the Château d'Audrieu

Country roads lead back to Caen, the starting point for this route. If thoughts are turning to the next meal, then a small detour to **Audrieu** (south of the RN13 halfway between Bayeux and Caen may resolve the issue of where to eat. **Château d'Audrieu** (tel: 31 80 21 52, fax: 31 80 24 73) is an 18th-century country house, now a hotel with a celebrated four-star restaurant. The standard of accommodation is high, as are the prices.

Route 13

Pure Normandy:
A tour round the coast of the Cotentin Peninsula
(354km/220 miles)

It sometimes seems as if the people of this region have had more than their fair share of misfortune. Their old farmhouses and homes sometimes resemble mini-fortresses hastily erected from rough stones. Farmers' bumpy fields often extend to within a stone's throw of the sea, so that their crops get a salty tang even before they are harvested. No point on the Cotentin Peninsula lies further than 50km (30 miles) from the coast and this proximity to the sea has made its mark on the people and shaped their character. Some similarities with Brittany are quite striking: wind-battered coasts, trees bowed by Atlantic storms and stone-wall field enclosures. Practically everywhere on the Cotentin Peninsula a fresh wind blows, a free, health-enhancing bonus to every holiday.

Three days is the minimum period required for this route with stops in Cherbourg and Granville recommended. Both towns are well equipped for summer's tourist influx. As well as being a major Channel port, Cherbourg (*see page 69*) is the rail terminus for Paris St-Lazare main line via Lisieux, Caen, Bayeux and Carentan. Bus services operated by the STN company connect Cherbourg with St-Lô via Barfleur, St-Vaast-la-Hougue and Carentan.

Granville (*see page 72*) is the rail terminus for trains from Paris via Dreux and Argentan. The line from Caen to Rennes passes through Folligny, 16km (10 miles) east of Granville. Bus services operated by the STN company connect Granville with Coutances and with Mont St-Michel via Avranches.

Cherbourg is a major Channel port

67

A couple of sea dogs

St-Lô: remains of the town wall

Tempting sign in Carentan

Ste-Marie-du-Mont

Reminders of the Longest Day on Utah Beach

Sights

St-Lô (pop. 26,500) is the administrative centre of the Manche *département*. It lies on a hill above the Vire Valley and makes an excellent start and finish to this tour. Despite its importance within the region, it is not a town usually on the tourist's itinerary. This probably results from the fact that around 90 percent of the town was destroyed during World War II. Only the remains of the old town, known as **l'Enclos**, were left and just the southern wall of the town was rebuilt after the war. The church of **Notre-Dame**, built between the 13th and 17th century, suffered the loss of both its towers, although a late Gothic external pulpit survived.

The 'town of ruins' has, however, retained its reputation for horse-breeding and the **Haras de St-Lô** stud (open mid-July to the beginning of March) owes its existence to Napoleon. Public performances, including demonstrations of working horses take place every Thursday at 10am between the end of July and the beginning of September.

Carentan (pop. 7,500) is often described as the 'Gateway to the Cotentin'. It plays an important part in the regional beef and dairy cattle trade. Every Monday the local farmers bring their stock to the cattle market. The central **Place de la République** with its row of old houses makes an attractive focal point and the pretty 15th-century arcades provide shade and shelter from the sun in the summer months.

The quickest route to the coast is via **Ste-Marie-du-Mont**, but a detour via **Ste-Mère-Eglise**, the first town to be liberated by the Allies, will shed light on an unusual war-time episode. John Steele, an American paratrooper, found himself entangled around the church spire as he landed and was not released for several hours. The **Musée des Troupes Aéroportées** (summer, 9am–6pm; 15 November to 15 December, 10am–noon, 2–6pm; closed 15 December to 15 January) includes among its exhibits photographs of the occasion, a cargo-carrying glider and other equipment.

The distinctive Cotentin coastal landscape begins with **Utah Beach** near **La Madeleine**. If storm clouds are looming on the distant horizon, then the wide, flat belts of sand with marram grass dunes can resemble paintings by Boudin. In summer this strip of beach becomes a racetrack for sand yachting enthusiasts. It can be fun to watch as the brightly-coloured buggies speed through the shallow water driven by the stiff breeze.

Utah Beach has a gruesome past. Monuments, memorial plaques, howitzers and military vehicles by the roadside are all reminders of the 'Longest Day'. In a bunker half-hidden by sand dune is the **Musée du Débarquement**. The wide range of exhibits helps to paint a comprehensive picture of the battles which accompanied the Allied forces' landing.

In contrast the old harbour at **St-Vaast-La-Hougue** (pop. 2,100) can only be described as idyllic. Holiday makers can relax, ignore the long shadows of war, take a sip of Calvados and enjoy the sight of brightly-painted boats bobbing up and down in the sun. St-Vaast is well known throughout France as the source of fine oysters. **Fort de la Hougue** lies in a military zone and is not accessible to the public, but the fortifications on the Ile Tatihou out in the bay may be visited, although there is a limit of 500 visitors per day (June to October, 10am–5pm). The old, restored fortress is used mainly for exhibitions and various cultural events.

St-Vaast-La-Hougue

On a fine day, **Barfleur** (pop. 599) with its huge stone houses by a sheltered harbour could easily be confused with the set of a maritime adventure film, but the fishing nets and piles of lobster pots left to dry on the quayside are proof that this is a busy working fishing port. The small, 17th-century fortified church has clearly withstood the full force of the winter storms. Barfleur's craftsmen have earned the town more than a footnote in the history books. They built many of the ships which took William's army across the English Channel in 1066. In 1194, after his adventures in the Middle East and Europe, Richard I sailed from here home to England.

Bustling Barfleur

Just north of Barfleur, country lanes lead down to the coast. At **Pointe de Saire**, a make-shift café offers welcome refreshments and a chance to watch the seagulls' aerobatic displays. Near Gatteville-le-Phare, the **Pointe de Barfleur** Peninsula juts out into the English Channel and the platform of the 71-m (240-ft) lighthouse offers a fine viewing point over the countryside. In the centre of **Tocqueville** stands a bust of the famous statesman and historian Alexis de Tocqueville (*see page 84*), whose family home lies on the edge of the village behind some tall trees.

On the outskirts of Cherbourg is **Tourlaville** Castle, the scene of a tragic series of events at the beginning of the 17th century. Thirteen-year-old Marguerite de Ravelet was forced by her parents to marry a man of 45 who cruelly mistreated her. She fled to Paris, seeking refuge with her student brother, but out of vengeance, the abandoned husband accused the two of incest and they were both beheaded on 2 December 1603.

The sea is in the locals' blood

The town of **Cherbourg** (pop. 92,000), at the northern tip of the Cotentin Peninsula, is often quickly bypassed by travellers to and from Portsmouth, Southampton and Poole, but if time is available a tour of the town can prove interesting, especially to plant-lovers and gardeners. Most

Parc Emmanuel-Liais

St-Trinité

70

The Théâtre on Place de Gaulle

visitors are surprised to find the **Parc Emmanuel-Liais** where the displays of azalea and rhododendron are particularly striking in spring. Other sub-tropical species such as camellia thrive in the mild, coastal climate.

Cherbourg is, of course, an important naval base and home to the French submarine fleet. Foreign nationals are not permitted to visit the **Arsenal**, from where France's first nuclear submarine was launched.

Naval vessels and channel ferries no longer monopolise the offshore waters. For several years yachts and motor-boats have moored in the marina at **Port Chantereyne**. In **Place Napoléon**, Emperor Napoleon I sits on a bronze horse nearby, pointing tellingly in the direction of England, the country which proved so defiant during the Napoleonic wars.

The basilica of **St-Trinité** in Rue de l'Eglise stands on the site of an earlier church. Its construction and ornamentation is characterised more by Flamboyant than Gothic influences. The altar is baroque, but the tower dates from 1825. However, the main interior attractions are 400-year-old decorations on the upper gallery of the nave. The painted carvings depict scenes from the life of Jesus.

Tuesday and Thursday are market days and the farmers and fishermen meet under the colourful marquees in the **Place de Gaulle**. The tables are invariably weighed down with mounds of fruit and vegetables, smoked hams and mouth-watering tartlets. The neo-baroque facade of the late 19th-century **Théâtre** forms the imposing backdrop for the market scene. Behind the theatre, the **Musée Thomas-Henry** (daily except Monday, 9am–noon, 2–6pm) houses works by Jean-François Millet (1814–75), Hubert Robert (1733–1808) and the Italian artist Angelico (c. 1387–1455).

The **Fort du Roule** on a 100-m (325-ft) hilltop looks down over the rooftops and the view gives a clear picture of Cherbourg's geographical location and an insight into its commercial activities. Against the background of a choppy English Channel, wide avenues, apartment blocks and industrial complexes dominate the foreground. The **Musée de la Guerre et la Libération** whose exhibits document the Allied landing is to be found in the ramparts.

Every Wednesday and Saturday in July and August, there are organised walks around Chebourg starting from the town's tourist office.

The road out of Cherbourg to the west heads towards the remotest point in Normandy. Television aerials on rooftops and cars parked beside houses in tiny hamlets surrounded by bleak, hilly countryside are the only signs that the 20th century has reached this part of France. Fresh winds chase the clouds across the broad bay between **Urville-**

Nacqueville and **Landemer**. Walkers can follow a rough track towards **Cap de la Hague** and the lighthouse finally marks the weather-beaten tip of the continent. The plots of closely-cropped grass and houses made of rough stone, sometimes lying in gentle dips are reminiscent of scenes from southern Ireland.

Cap de la Hague

The less forbidding west coast of the Cotentin peninsula begins at the cape. The deserted **Baie d'Ecalgrain** with its grey sand and black granite curves round beneath the green meadows. The 127-m (416-ft) **Nez de Jobourg**, Europe's highest cliff, juts out like a church pulpit. The winding coast road leads south through **Herqueville** revealing a fine view of the pretty **Anse de Vauville** bay.

Anse de Vauville

The little town of **Biville** has two surprises for the unsuspecting traveller. First, there is the 12th-century church where a marble sarcophagus enclosing the glass coffin of the Blessed Thomas Hélye lies. A pilgrimage to the church takes place on 18–19 October. Second, there is the undulating dune landscape beneath the church.

As the coastline winds its way south towards Mont St-Michel, the distance between high and low water increases. The greatest difference recorded in Normandy is 14m (45ft), exceeded only by the Bay of Fundy in Canada. The little port of **Diélette** is the best place to observe this phenomenon. At low tide fishing boats rest in pools of seawater like beached whales.

Low tide at Diélette

The towns of **Carteret** and **Barneville-Carteret** are firmly established tourist resorts. The coastal path here is part of the long-distance GR223 Footpath, known as the *Sentier des Douaniers* (Customs Officers' Path).

Lessay lies inland at the mouth of the Ay Estuary. Visitors to the town are inevitably drawn to the early Romanesque **monastery church** of the former Benedictine abbey (daily, 8am–7pm, guided tours in the summer months at 11am and 3pm). Despite severe damage during World War II, the original stones were used in the restoration work and the church was reconsecrated in 1958. On the second weekend in September, the sleepy, country town is aroused from its slumbers. Ever since the 13th century, the Holy Cross market has been held here, nowadays attracting traders, performers and hordes of visitors. While adults watch the dog and horse shows, roundabouts and swingboats keep the children entertained.

Château de Pirou

To one side of the main road **Château de Pirou** guards the surrounding area. This fortified castle was built 800 years ago to protect Coutances. A legend can perhaps explain the large number of geese to be seen nearby. When the Vikings finally took the castle they were astonished to find just an old man behind the walls. He told the Norsemen that all the other soldiers had turned into geese and flown

off and the Vikings said they remembered seeing a flock of geese flying overhead earlier on. Every year the geese return to the Cotentin Peninsula in the hope of finding the book with the instructions for changing them back into men, but the book will never be found as it was burnt by the Vikings during the siege of the castle.

In earlier times **Coutances** (pop. 13,000) was an important religious and spiritual centre. The old houses cluster around the famous ★★ **Cathédrale Notre-Dame**, one of the finest and purest examples of Norman Gothic. The first church was constructed before William acceded to the English throne. It was destroyed by fire in 1218 and rebuilt incorporating the ruins of its predecessor. As well as all the rich ornamentation, it is the sheer dimensions and precise geometry are very impressive. The effect of the light from the 60-m (196-ft) octagonal lantern tower is another striking feature.

Gothic marvel: Notre-Dame

For an authentic taste of Normandy visit the *boulangerie authentique* just south of the village of **Lingreville** by the junction of the D20 and D298. This is a traditional bakery adjoining a simple village café and the master baker is renowned for his traditional rustic bread. It is made from a mixture of flours and has a delicious crust. Brought into the house while still warm, a loaf will give off an irresistible, oven-fresh aroma.

En route to Lingreville

The resort of **Granville** (pop. 12,500) is overlooked by a huge rock which is visible from afar. Famed for its casino it is sometimes described as the 'Monaco of the north' and one of its most famous sons was the fashion designer, Christian Dior (1905–57). With its rusty anchor chains, lobster pots, nets, gleaming yachts and fishing boats, Granville is predominantly a fishing town, but in recent years tourism has been playing an increasingly important part in the town's economy.

Granville has an unusual past as, alone among Normandy's towns, it was founded by the English in the 15th century. The grand plan was to create a base from which to capture Mont St-Michel, but the scheme foundered and the English were forced to flee after only three years. A walled upper town, now referred to as the **Haute Ville**, grew up on the rock and successfully kept attackers at bay for many centuries. A drawbridge by the **Grand'Porte** allows access to the ramparts from the port. The view from the hill extends inland over the walls and rooftops. In the other direction, the **Iles Chausey** and Mont St-Michel can be seen on the horizon.

Grand'Porte

At the western end of the upper town, a lighthouse on the **Pointe du Roc** marks the northern boundary of St-Michael's Bay.

Route 14

Wonder of the modern world:
Granville – ★★★ Mont St-Michel (60km/37 miles)

Like a ghost ship under sail, a pyramid emerges from the mist. This monastery on a rock is certainly the best known of Normandy's sights; some describe it as one of the wonders of the western world and few are disappointed by what they find. While steeped in its own history, what makes it such an attractive destination is its commanding position on the mud-flats of the Baie du Mont St-Michel.

Avranches (*see page 74*) lies on the Caen–Rennes railway line. A service links Avranches with Mont St-Michel (*see page 75*) and Granville. The nearest station to Mont St-Michel is at Pontorson, but there is a regular bus services linking the two towns.

Sights

The coast road from Granville passes first through the village of **St-Pair-sur-Mer**, after St Paterne (or Saint-Pair) who founded a monastery there in AD540 and set about converting the people to Christianity. The church has an early Romanesque tower and St-Pair's tomb lies in the 14th-century chancel.

Kairon-Plage is a windsurfers' paradise and a little further south lies the pleasant resort of **Julouville**.

The village of **Carolles** with its fine beaches to the north makes a good starting point for short walks. Inland lies the green **Vallée des Peintres** and the GR223, a long-distance footpath, follows the coast as far as **Le Pignon Butor** where a magnificent clifftop view extends north to Granville Rock. From Carolles the cliffs become steeper

Mont St-Michel viewed from the Jardin des Plantes

and the view of the distant Mont St-Michel becomes clearer. On a fine day the view from the **Pointe de Champeaux** is superb.

Avranches town walls

Avranches (pop. 10,500) is the largest town in the **Baie du Mont St-Michel** and its history is closely linked with the famous monastery. Bishop Aubert founded a monastery here in the 8th century, but even in the preceding centuries, especially during the Roman occupation, Avranches had been an administrative centre. It was to be taken later by Anglo-Saxons, then by Franks and finally by the Vikings. From the 10th century onwards, strong fortifications were constructed but only the **Tour Baudange** and **Tour de l'Arsenal** remain and can be found behind the town hall below the keep.

The central square makes a good starting point for a tour of the town, especially as the **tourist office** is situated there and it supplies street plans. On the north side of the square, a signposted flight of steps leads to the **Palais Episcopal** (Bishop's Palace). Built in the 15th century the building has been restored a number of times and the highlight is the foyer with ribbed vaulting. The ★★ **Musée Municipal d'Avranches** occupies some rooms in the nearby Tribunal de l'Officialité. Exhibits include a fine collection of illuminated manuscripts.

Musée Municipal, exhibit

74

From the museum the walk passes the old deanery (26 rue de l'Auditoire) to an open space known as the **Plateforme**. The cathedral of St-André was constructed here in the 12th century, but collapsed in 1794. Three other churches have occupied the site, the oldest of which was built in the 5th century. A slab at the door of the cathedral reminds visitors that an event of great historical importance took place here on 11 May, 1172. Henry II, King of England, kneeled barefoot in the white robe of a penitent, to offer his public apologies for his part in the murder of Thomas Becket, the Archbishop of Canterbury.

Rue de Lille heads back towards the town centre and is lined by a number of Renaissance houses formerly used by the cathedral clergy.

Follow the medieval cobbles in **Rue Engibault** to the **Maison Bergevin**. This house in a cul-de-sac forms a part of the city wall and is worth a quick look. Around **Rue Pomme d'Or** in the direction of church of St-Gervais lies the old business and artisans' quarter. Pass the 17th-century **Maison aux Gargouilles** (Gargoyle House) in Rue Challemel-Lacour to reach the market square or **Place du Marché**, which is bordered by several historic houses.

In the church of **St-Gervais** with its 74-m (242-ft) grey granite bell-tower, the skull of Bishop Aubert can be seen. The dent in the bone is said to have been made by the Archangel Michael who had ordered him in a dream to build a chapel on Mont St-Michel. Initially the bishop was unsure of the message, whereupon the Archangel appeared twice more. On the third occasion, to ensure that the instruction was quite clear, he tapped the bishop on the head leaving behind a thumbprint.

From the church, cross Place St-Aubert and head back towards the town hall. Southwest of the town hall and outside the scope of the walk lies the **Jardin des Plantes**. Not only do these botanical gardens contain some unusual plants, but the panorama over Mount St Michael's Bay from the gardens of this old Capuchin monastery should not be missed.

Jardin des Plantes

★★★ **Mont St-Michel** (summer 9.30am–6pm; winter 9.30–11.45am, 1.45–4.15pm; closed 1 January, 1 May, 11 November and 25 December; the monastery itself may only be viewed as part of a conducted tour taking in the abbey buildings, St Aubert's Chapel, the abbey church, the church of Notre-Dame-sous-Terre, the Merveille and the magnificent cloister).

If a piece of heaven landed on earth, then it was Mont St-Michel. This monastery perched on a rocky island in a desert of sand stands as a timeless monument to human hopes and aspirations. Centuries ago pilgrims flocked here from all corners of Europe to save their souls – at that spot where heaven and earth seemed closer together than anywhere else on earth and neither poverty nor frailty prevented the faithful from making the journey.

And today? This illuminated fortress of faith which glows in the darkness like a beacon has lost none of its awe-inspiring dignity and greatness. As soon as day dawns in the east over Avranches, the first cars and coaches start to move across the causeway. 'God's Pyramid' becomes

Today's pilgrims

'God's Pyramid'

75

Battlements of Mont St-Michel

Archangel Michael

an ant-hill overrun by tourists. Hundreds of thousands visit every year, but the numbers who visit in search of divine consolation or religious fulfilment are few. At the end of another long day the steep and narrow alleys empty and the car park becomes just another section of sandy beach.

It was just a rough rocky outcrop 900m (2,950ft) long and 78m (255ft) high, when in AD708 – so the legend goes – Aubert, the bishop of Avranches, was instructed in a dream by the Archangel Michael to build an oratory or small chapel at the summit. Many years after Aubert's death in 966, a Benedictine monastery was founded there at the insistence of the then Duke of Normandy, Richard I. Thirty monks first built a pre-Romanesque church over the oratory. This was later to form the **Notre-Dame-sous-Terre** (Our Lady below Ground) when an enlargement of the church above reduced its status to a crypt. The consecration of the abbey church in the 11th century completed the first phase.

The second phase started in 1180 and lasted for a further 20 years, involving the construction of a monastery in Romanesque style, a residence for the abbot, a refectory, guests' hall and almshouse. The third and grandest phase in Gothic style started at the beginning of the 13th century. The architects set about creating ★★ **La Merveille** (the Marvel), the east and west wings of the monastery, justifiably described as an architectural masterpiece. Two storeys of this building were to consist of a guests' hall and knights' hall, while the refectory and ★★ **cloister** occupied the third floor. By the time this final phase was completed, Mont St-Michel had become one of the most sacred places in the whole of France, but it took on a new role as a military abbey. A garrison was stationed here and increasing attention had to be given to fortifications. In the 15th century English troops mounted an unsuccessful assault on the monastery.

76

The cloister

More alterations were made, followed by a less strict regime for the monks. Slowly the monastery declined in importance, a process which was accelerated by the French Revolution. In 1863 it was converted into a prison and it was only in the final years of the 19th century that the pointed steeple was added to the abbey church.

Today, Mont St-Michel draws in excess of 1.5 million visitors a year. In high season the massive car park is always full. The smell of sugared *crêpes* or spicy *merguez* sausages dominates the Grande Rue, where crowds throng in and out of the souvenir shops. The route to the summit leads through the **Porte de l'Avancée** main entrance, up the **Grande Rue** along the ramparts to the **Grand Degré** steps, but if you prefer to wait for the coach parties to disperse, a stroll around the huge rock underneath the ramparts can be very rewarding.

No shortage of souvenirs

Route 15

**Foundrymen and coppersmiths with Swiss accents:
Mont St-Michel – Suisse Normande – Orne Valley –
Caen (150km/93 miles)**

Rolling countryside generally characterises Normandy but
there are one or two hilly regions of which the **Suisse Normande** is the most popular. Swiss Normandy lies just south
of Caen. This delightful valley has been carved by the
River Orne and has created an area ideal for such activities as walking, mountaineering, canoeing or cycling. To
make a comparison with Switzerland is an overstatement,
but the attractions of the region's contours with no hill
higher than 365m (1,200ft) are varied and impressive.

The nearest train stations to Clécy (*see page 78*) are at
Caen and Flers. There are bus services connecting Caen,
Thury-Harcourt, Clécy, Condé-sur-Noireau and Flers.

Sights

Starting out from Mont St-Michel (*see page 73*) head first
for **Villedieu-les-Poêles** (pop. 4,300) via Avranches (*see
page 74*). This typically Norman town enjoys a reputation
as a centre of the metalworking trade. A quick stroll
through the narrow streets will provide a clear indication
of the type of goods produced here: saucepans, frying pans,
kettles – all made of copper. Most of these items, which
are mainly of decorative value, are made at the **Atelier du
Cuivre** (54 rue du Général-Huard, tel: 33 51 31 85, fax:
33 51 04 96; weekdays 9am–noon, 2–5pm). Perhaps of
greater interest is the local bell-foundry which continues
to use the traditional methods. The ★ **Fondrerie de
Cloches** (Rue du Pont-Chignon, tel: 33 61 00 56, fax: 33

Villedieu-les-Poêles

77

Copper is a local speciality

Tour de l'Horloge in Vire

90 02 99; daily 8am–noon, 2–6pm – please phone first if intending to visit on Sunday and Monday between September and June) makes bells of all sizes in its old workshop. Many are exported through the world. The nearby church of **Notre-Dame**, not far from the foundry, dates from the 15th century and is admired for its impressive late Gothic style.

The symbol of **Vire** (pop. 15,000) is the **Tour de l'Horloge** in the town centre. The lower section dates from the 13th century and a belltower was added some 200 years later. The tower is one of the few old buildings in the town which survived World War II unscathed. In a loop on the River Vire and accessible from the Place du Château stand the ruins of a **keep**. It was built in 1123 by Henri I Beauclerc and affords a fine view over the valley. The town grew up on a textile industry and its bawdy workers' songs were called *Vaux de Vire*, said to be the origin of the word 'Vauderville'.

A detour to **La-Ferrière-Harang** about 20km (12 miles) north of Vire will reward those with a dare-devil streak. The bridge over the River Soulevre claims to be the original European bungee-jumping centre, started by a New Zealander, and it remains a favourite launching pad for fearless jumpers.

Clécy, on the other hand, the 'capital' of Swiss Normandy, offers other more orthodox sporting activities. Brightly-coloured canoes and kayaks can often be seen on the stretch of river between Clécy and Pont d'Ouilly. As well as plenty of short walks two long-distance routes pass nearby: GR36 Ouistreham to Ecouché (145km/90 miles) and GR221 Pont d'Ouilly to Bény-Bocage (52km/32 miles). Other activities include: riding, hang-gliding in St-Omer, golf, sailing, flying, gliding, climbing, mountaineering and fishing.

A day-long tour of the region starting from Clécy is signposted as the **Route de la Suisse Normande**, but historic buildings, picturesque town centres or interesting museums are in short supply – the distinguishing features of the tour are the rustic charm and peaceful countryside, ideal for walkers, cyclists and outdoor pursuits enthusiasts. At **St-Rémy** the route leaves behind the narrow Orne Valley and winds its way up the sun-bathed hillsides to the **Route des Crêtes**. The Crests' Road heads east over the undulating plain to **St-Omer**, the only place where other traffic may slow progress. Above the cliffs at **Rochers de la Houle** nature has created a perfect take-off point for hang-gliders.

Thury-Harcourt (pop. 1,800) is the northern gate to Swiss Normandy and, like Clécy, it has in recent years become a busy tourist centre with hotels, bars and shops. The

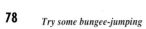

Try some bungee-jumping

Enjoying an aerial view

town's name derives from the Harcourts who built their family residence here at the beginning of the 18th century. The duke's castle was burnt down in 1944 with only the ruins now left standing in splendid parkland. On summer days it is pleasant to make the 5-km (3-mile) walk through the grounds. At the northern edge of the town the Orne loops round cutting between steep rocks to create the **Boucle du Hom** and walkers can follow a path along the banks of the river here. The main road to Caen leaves the river valley in the town and Caen lies 26km (16 miles) to the northeast.

Boucle du Hom

For a pleasant detour sweeping round the Orne Valley in an arc, start in the west at **Mont-Pinçon** (365m/1,200ft), the region's highest peak. Near a lake fed by the River Druance stands the 16th-century **Château de Pontécoulant** and the Musée Départementale.

Admiral Dumont d'Urville was a famous son of the little town of **Condé-sur-Noireau**. He was born in 1790 and among the most famous of his exploits was the well-documented exploration of lands in the South Pacific including New Guinea, New Zealand and the Antarctic. A memorial to the seafarer stands in the town's Place de l' Hôtel de Ville. The stones at the foot of the monument were brought back from the Antarctic by a fellow explorer.

Follow the river Noireau as far as **Pont d'Ouilly** on the River Orne, now one of Suisse Normande's principal resorts. Although rebuilt and modernised after the war, along the valley there is evidence of an earlier age when spinning and tanning were the local industries. Return to Clécy via **Le Bô**.

79

Château de Pontécoulant and interior detail

Art History

Normandy's genius has shaped French and even world culture, in three areas – architecture, literature and art.

Architecture

During the first one thousand years of modern times the architecture of Normandy was influenced chiefly by the Romans and then the Scandinavian Vikings, but from the middle of the 11th century, a distinctly independent style evolved. Admittedly, early Romanesque influences of the Burgundian school were adopted, but a distinctive Norman style soon emerged. Fine examples exist in the Romanesque abbey at Jumièges Monastery as well as the Romanesque galleried basilica at the Church of St-Etienne in Caen. Rounded arches in the interior; a gallery with openings to the central nave; a facade with twin towers and a tower above the crossing on a rectangular ground plan. These were to become the typical features of Norman style – a style which was even 'exported' abroad. London's Westminster Abbey, built between 1050 and 1065 by Edward the Confessor, still serves to illustrate the talents of the architect, who had, in fact, spent some time in exile in Normandy. One of the most striking features of Norman architecture is the fact that the strict rules for building in stone that had applied until then were cast aside. Thick, solid walls which had previously borne the weight of the roof were replaced by buttresses – allowing the entry of light – and ribbed vaults, two features which pointed clearly towards the next development of the style into Gothic.

Slender columns are typical Gothic features

81

The first Gothic building was the Eglise St-Denis in Ile de France built by Abbot Suger in the middle of the 12th century. This style soon spread throughout Europe. And yet certain elements, such as the lantern tower above the crossing, were unique to Normandy. One such example is the lantern tower, apparently made of engraved stone, in Coutances Cathedral. Even during the Romanesque period architects sought to allow as much daylight as possible through the crossing tower to illuminate the otherwise gloomy interior and they often placed the altar at a focal point for daylight. During the Gothic era many major sacred buildings were built in Normandy and the decorations became even more ornate, culminating in the extravagant late Gothic Flamboyant style. Notre-Dame Cathedral and the St-Ouen Church in Rouen are superb examples, as is the Church of Notre-Dame in Pont-de-l'Arche.

Flamboyant style in St-Ouen

The French term 'flamboyant' means 'flaming', as the tracery of the bays and rose windows are said to resemble flickering flames.

Géricault was both painter and sculptor

Rouen Cathedral by Monet

Claude Monet House

Painting

Théodore Géricault (1791–1824) was one of the first native Norman artists and sculptors. Born in Rouen he was an important influence on French Romantic art. He began his career copying old masters such as Rubens and Titian, but his unorthodox approach and bold use of colour incurred the disapproval of his teacher. He first came to the public's attention with an exhibition piece entitled *Officer of Light Horse* at the Salon of 1812. Seven years later he produced his masterpiece *The Raft of Medusa*, based on a shipwreck which had just caused a sensation in France. Towards the end of his life he painted five portraits of the insane.

In the year Géricault died, Eugène Boudin (1824–98) was born in Honfleur. His best known works are seascapes, including *Deauville* and *Harbour of Trouville*. He was a precursor of the Impressionist movement, which started in the 1860s, reaching its climax between 1870 and 1880. The best known exponents of Impressionism include Claude Monet, Camille Pissarro, Auguste Renoir, Alfred Sisley, Jean Frédérick Bazille and, at times, Edgar Degas and Paul Cézanne.

It was Claude Monet (1840–1926) who provided the impetus for this celebrated movement. His family moved from Paris to Le Havre when he was eight and there he met Eugène Boudin, who encouraged him to paint in the open air. One day he painted a picture of the harbour, *Impression: Soleil Levant*. When he exhibited in Paris in 1874 it gained one critic's derision as *Impressioniste*. He met Camille Pissarro while studying in Paris, and a few years later he became acquainted with Renoir, Sisley and Bazille

and they worked together. The aim of this circle of artists was to convey on canvas the nuances, as they saw them, of natural colour and light.

Monet settled at Giverny near Vernon in 1883. The country house with a garden that he laid out himself was to be his home until he died more then 40 years later. Occasionally he made excursions into the nearby country-side and even to London and Venice. Portrayed in the changing intensity of daylight, *Rouen Cathedral* (1894) is one of his most famous works. During the later years of his life, however, he rarely ventured outside his own magnificent garden where he loved painting the colourful flowerbeds and the water-lily pond.

While Monet was a Norman only by choice, native Norman painters include Raoul Dufy (1877–1953) and Emile Othon Friesz (1879–1949), both of whom came from Le Havre. Ferdinand Léger (1881–1955) was a native of Argentan. Pissarro and Georges Braque, the master of Cubism, both ended their days in Normandy.

Literature

In the Middle Ages it became possible to talk of Norman literature. Writers emerged at both the Duke of Normandy's court and in the many monasteries, which had developed from the 7th century onwards as religious and spiritual centres. This early literature dealt primarily with historical themes. The Jumièges monk, Guillaume Caillouwie, wrote *The History of the Vikings* and Guillaume de Poitiers, the archdeacon of Lisieux, wrote a discourse in Latin on William II, Duke of Normandy and King of England. Also using Latin, Guy de Ponthieu documented the famous Battle of Hastings in 1066.

In the early 13th century when Normandy and France united the region began to lose some of its identity, but in the ensuing centuries it was nevertheless home to many world famous writers. One of France's greatest playwrights, Pierre Corneille (1606–84) was born in Rouen and, having worked initially as a lawyer for the king, published his first comedy at the age of 23. After the tremendous success of his first work, in 1637 he published the tragi-comedy *El Cid* – a controversial play, and one of the most important works of the 17th century.

Gustave Flaubert, born in Rouen in 1821, ranks as one of Normandy's literary masters. The son of a doctor, he reluctantly studied law at Paris, where his friendship with Maxime du Camp, Victor Hugo, and Louise Colet who became his lover, stimulated his already apparent talent for writing. Soon after finishing his studies, he was afflicted by a nervous disease which may have been partly responsible for the morbidity and pessimism revealed in his first masterpiece, *Madame Bovary*, the tale of a bourgeois

83

Flaubert

Madame Bovary Museum in Ry

romance. After its publication in 1857, Flaubert was accused of offending public morality but was later acquitted. In his writings Flaubert fought against the use of banal everyday language, against clichés and platitudes, resisting attempts to debase the French language.

Flaubert enjoyed a close friendship with the third great Norman writer, Guy de Maupassant (1850–93). He came from near Fécamp and worked for several years as a government clerk but encouraged by Flaubert he took to writing. Early lyrical and dramatic works were overshadowed by his first success, *Boule de Suif*, in 1880, which was then followed by a highly productive decade. He wrote six novels, numerous travel guides and about 260 short stories before he fell victim to mental illness in 1892 and died two years later.

Alexis de Tocqueville

Another Norman who achieved fame for his writings was Alexis de Tocqueville (1805–59), who specialised in the realm of historical and political analysis. A man of aristocratic background from the north of the Cotentin Peninsula, he travelled to the USA and made a study of the American political system. His shrewd conclusions, published in 1835 as *De la Démocratie en Amérique*, quickly established his reputation. He later became active in politics, reaching the post of French foreign minister. Having dedicated the last years of his life to writing historical and political works he died in Cannes in 1859.

Among other French writers who found inspiration on the Normandy coast, Marcel Proust (1871–1922) is probably the best known. He was a frequent visitor to the coastal resorts and for health reasons, between 1881 and 1893, he spent many weeks taking the sea air.

Festivals

Jan/February	Fair in Caen.
February	Carnival in Caen.
March	Sausage market in Mortagne-au-Perche.
April	Antiques market in L'Aigle.
May	Jazz festival in Coutances; May festival in Evreux; international hockey tournament in Deauville with regatta on the English Channel; Normandy festival in Etretat; Joan of Arc festival in Rouen; seaman's festival in Honfleur; procession of the Brotherhood of Mercy in Bernay; international regatta in Cherbourg; surfing competition at Cap d'Antifer.

Joan of Arc

June	Literary festival in Forges-les-Eaux; International festival of romantic films in Cabourg; ballooning festival in Balleroy; June festival in Verneuil-sur-Avre; Pilgrimage on Trinity Sunday in Fécamp.
July	Jazz festival and horse-racing in Deauville; international folk festival in Domfront; pilgrimage to Mont St-Michel; festival of classical music in Honfleur; jazz festival in Trouville; festival of the sea in Fécamp; clown fair and horse show in Forges-les-Eaux; fireworks in Lisieux; historical festival in Carrouges; bridge tournament in Deauville; pilgrimage to Mont St-Michel.

85

Mont St-Michel

August	Polo world championship; festival of the sea and painting festival in Yport; 'La Fanatic Cup' windsurfing competition in Cabourg; festival of the sea in St-Vaast-la-Hougue; pilgrimage in Lisieux; son-et-lumière in Forges-les-Eaux.
September	St Theresa's festival in Lisieux; Holy Cross market in Lessay; American film festival in Deauville; international fair in Caen; international hang-gliding convention in Dieppe; St Michael's pilgrimage at Mont St-Michel.

Hang-gliding Convention

October	Vintage car rally in Deauville; horse-racing and parade in Haras-du-Pin; apple fair in Vimoutiers.
November	Herring fair in Lieurey and in Dieppe; cider festival in Beuvron-en-Auge; St-Romain fair in Rouen; St-Martin fair in Neufchâtel-en-Bray.
December	Turkey festival in Sées; St Nicholas market in Evreux.

Food and Drink

Take a stroll through one of Normandy's many weekly markets, but be ready to exercise a little self-control. The appetising selection of cheese, fish, vegetables and meat will certainly arouse your taste buds, but the visual effect can be quite stunning too. Regard these markets as a challenge – many of the delights on offer will be hard to resist.

Livarot cheese

Norman cuisine takes no account of calorie charts. Butter, cream and Calvados have a permanent place next to the cooker. Double cream, sometimes even triple cream, is often used to enrich sauces – it supplies many dishes with that full, unmistakeable taste of Normandy.

The fishing tradition ensures that menus can include turbot, skate, monkfish, sole, carp, sea trout and salmon. Seafood is also plentiful with crabs, scallops, mussels, prawns and oysters often served together as *fruits de mer*. On the Cotentin Peninsula in particular, the custom of dripping a little lemon juice on to oysters is frowned upon. Instead, in St-Vaast and elsewhere, the precious molluscs are served with a shallot and apple vinegar sauce. For those who prefer their seafood cooked, try *Huîtres aux Pommes*. The shelled oysters are served *au gratin* on slightly sour apples. *Marmite Dieppoise* is a fish soup cooked in the Dieppe style with a creamy sauce.

Abundance of seafood

87

But fish and seafood are not the only main courses. *Agneau Pré-salé* is often found and is a dish made from lambs, which have been fed on the grass of the salty meadows along the Normandy coast. Offal dishes such as *Tripes à la mode de Caen* are also popular. *Soupe à la Graisse* (dripping soup) consists of several types of vegetables, including leek, cabbage, green beans, celery and parsley, cooked with plenty of dripping.

The symbol of the *département* of Calvados is, of course, the world renowned apple brandy which bears the same name. The ratio between sweet and sour apples for the unfermented juice is kept a well-guarded secret. The juice can be described as *cidre bouché* when an alcohol content of 5 percent is reached and this type of apple wine, which can be bought in bottles, is served throughout Normandy. Like wine the taste and quality can vary enormously. The unfermented juice which is made into Calvados stays in the barrel on its yeast for two years, and it is then distilled in stages until an alcohol content of 25 percent is attained. Storage in oak casks gives what would otherwise be a colourless liquid an amber tint. Calvados which is two years old is described as *vieux*, after three years, the producer may call it *vieille réserve* and after six years *hors d'âge*. Other liquid delights include *Pommeau*, an 18 percent apple liqueur and *Bénédictine*, a herb-flavoured liqueur from Fécamp.

Calvados in oak casks

Charcuterie delights, Bayeux

Restaurant selection

The following is a selection of recommended restaurants in Normandy's major centres.

Avranches: Le Menestrel, 37 boulevard du Luxembourg, tel: 33 58 12 20, fax: 33 58 40 11. The restaurant of Les Abrincates hotel offering good value menus.

Bayeux: Lion d'Or. The best cuisine in town. Speciality of the house is a type of black pudding known as *andouille*. Worth trying but not to everyone's taste. **L'Amaryllis**, 32 rue St-Patrice, tel: 31 22 47 94. Good, reasonably priced meals.

Cabourg: Les Dunes, Rue Léon Pican, tel: 31 24 38 00. Reservation recommended at this fish restaurant in the dunes. **Guillaume le Conquérant**, 2 rue Hastings in neighbouring Dives-sur-Mer, tel: 31 91 07 26. A 16th-century coach house, part of which is now a traditional-style restaurant.

Caen: Le Dauphin, 29 rue Gemare, tel: 31 86 22 26, fax: 31 86 35 14. An exquisitely furnished former monastery but inflated prices. **La Bourride**, 15 rue de Vaugueux, tel: 31 93 50 76, fax: 31 93 29 63. One of their specialities is called 'Symphony around an Apple' - it tastes as good as it sounds.

Caudebec-en-Caux: Manoir de Rétival, rue St-Clair, tel: 35 96 11 22, fax: 35 96 29 22. Sophisticated meat and fish dishes.

Cherbourg: Few top-class hotels are to be found in Cherbourg, but some restaurants produce good-quality regional specialities at reasonable prices. Try **Le Grandgousier**, 21 rue Abbaye, tel: 33 53 19 43 or **L'Ancre Dorée**, 27 rue Abbaye, tel: 33 93 98 38, fax: 33 93 22 36.

Deauville: Ciro's, Les Planches, tel: 31 88 18 10, fax: 31 98 66 71. Deauville's undisputed gastronomic citadel, situated on the promenade. **Le Spinnaker**, 52 rue Mirabeau, tel: 31 88 24 40, fax: 31 88 43 58. Top-quality fish and seafood restaurant. Traditional Norman cuisine with generous use of cider and Calvados.

Dieppe: La Présidence, 2 boulevard de Verdun, tel: 35 84 31 31, fax: 35 84 86 70. A hotel restaurant with a reputation for traditional French as well as regional *haute cuisine*. **Marmite Dieppoise**, 8 rue St-Jean, tel: 35 84 24 26. One of the house specialities is the famous local dish, after which the restaurant is named. For an extensive choice of small bars and restaurants, take a walk along the quai Henri IV near the ferry terminal. Many of them, such as **La Musardière** or **L'Armorique** specialise in seafood.

Etretat: Le Donjon, chemin de St-Clair, tel: 35 27 08 23, fax: 35 29 92 24. Superb view along the cliffs; **Les Roches Blanches**, terrasse Boudin, tel: 35 27 07 34. Traditional Normandy cuisine.

Evreux: Hôtel-Restaurant de France, 29 rue St-Thomas, tel: 32 39 09 25. Best establishment in the town with attractive garden by the River Iton. **Le Jardin d'Elodie**, 11 rue de la Harpe, tel: 32 38 08 66. Splendid view of the cathedral; **Le Café Français**, Place du Marché, tel: 32 33 53 60, fax: 32 38 60 17. Very pleasant atmosphere but high prices.

Gothic setting in Evreux

Forge-les-Eaux: Auberge du Beau Lieu on the D915, tel: 35 90 50 36, fax: 35 90 35 98. Norman specialities served *al fresco*; **Hôtel de la Paix**, 17 rue Neufchâtel, tel: 35 90 51 22, fax: 35 09 83 62. Tourist menus at reasonable prices. There are also a number of rooms available with half-board.

Granville: La Gentilhommière, 152 rue Couraye, tel: 33 50 17 99. Specialities include a stew made with Iles Chausey lobster; **Normandy Chaumière**, 20 rue Paul-Poirier, tel: 33 50 01 71, fax: 33 50 15 34. Option of eating *al fresco*.

Honfleur: L'Assiette Gourmande, Quai des Passagers, tel: 31 89 24 88, fax: 31 89 90 17. A meeting-place for

Al fresco in Honfleur

lovers of fine food. **L'Absinthe**, 10 quai Quarantaine, tel: 31 89 39 00, fax: 31 89 53 60. Ideal for summer evenings. **La Lieutenance**, 12 place Ste-Catherine, tel: 31 89 07 52. Solid Norman cuisine.

Le Havre: Le Petit Bedon, 39 rue L. Brindeau, tel: 35 41 36 81, fax: 35 21 09 24. Le Havre's top restaurant with matching prices. Closed for the first half of August. **Yves Page**, 7 place Clemenceau, Ste-Adresse, tel: 35 46 06 09. Seafood specialities.

Le Tréport: Hôtel-Restaurant **La Vieille Ferme** in Criel-sur-Mer west of Le Tréport, tel: 35 86 72 18, fax: 35 86 12 67. A picturesque farmhouse dating from 1734 serving traditional Norman cuisine. **Le Homard Bleu**, 45 quai François I, tel: 35 86 15 89, fax: 35 86 49 21. Square meals at reasonable prices.

Les Andelys: La Chaine d'Or, 27 rue Grande, tel: 32 54 00 31, fax: 32 54 05 68. Atmospheric hotel with restaurant offering excellent Norman cuisine in an 18th-century *auberge*.

Lisieux: Ferme du Roy, about 2km (1¼ miles) from the town on the road to Deauville, tel: 31 31 33 98. Best restaurant in the area set in an old farmhouse; **Aux Acacias**, 13 rue Résistance, tel: 31 62 10 95. Traditional cuisine. Central location. **France**, 5 rue au Char, tel: 31 62 03 37. Reasonably priced restaurant near Eglise St-Pierre.

Mont St-Michel: Mouton Blanc, tel: 33 60 14 08, fax: 33 60 05 62. Norman specialities.

Coffee-time in Rouen's Vieux-Marché

Rouen: Gill, 9 quai de la Bourse, tel: 35 71 16 14, fax: 35 71 96 91. Rouen's best restaurant. Specialities include puff pastry dishes or pigeon. **Couronne**, 31 place du Vieux-Marché, tel: 35 71 40 90, fax: 35 71 05 78. In one of Rouen's oldest town houses and one of several good restaurants in the square. **Les Nymphéas**, 9 rue de la Pie, tel: 35 89 26 69. A superb fish restaurant.

Vernon: Hôtel-Restaurant **Les Fleurs**, 71 rue Carnot, tel: 32 51 16 80, fax: 32 21 30 51. Regional cuisine. **La Gueulardière** 4km (2½ miles) outside the town in Port-Villez. Tel: 34 76 22 12. Cooking of a high standard and well worth a detour.

Clécy: Chalet de Chantepie, Clécy, tel: 31 69 71 10, fax: 31 69 66 72. Norman cuisine at decent prices; Relais de la Poste *(see above)*. The best place in town for a one-course dish or a meal with several courses.

Activity Holidays

A coastal location and open countryside make Normandy an ideal region for an activity holiday, especially those in or on the water. **Windsurfers** will inevitably make for those parts of the coast where the weather conditions are most favourable. The west coast of the Cotentin Peninsula: Kairon Plage, Plage de la Potinière near Barneville-Carteret, Le Rozel, Siouville. The north coast of the Cotentin Peninsula: Urville-Nacqueville. Calvados: Côte Fleurie (windsurfing is sometimes restricted at busy times). Côte d'Albâtre: Cap d'Antifer, Etretat, Ste-Marguerite, Mer-les-Bains near Le Tréport.

Utah Beach

Utah Beach on the east coast of the Cotentin Peninsula has developed into a popular place for **sand yachting** as the flat beach and prevailing wind direction provide the right conditions for the sport. All the equipment can be hired locally (Camping Le Cormoran, Ravenoville/Ste-Mère-Eglise, tel: 33 41 33 94, beginning of April to the end of September). There about 50 **sailing clubs** on the coast which hire out sailing boats (eg Noroit Marine, P. Delagree, 1 rue Destrais, F-50100 Tourlaville, tel: 33 20 30 64), as well as a number of sailing schools (eg Aries Location, J. Sauneuf, Port Chaterney, F-50100 Cherbourg, tel: 33 94 15 50; Jeune Araine, Dominique de Recy, 13 rue du Nord, F-50400 Granville, tel: 33 50 12 33).

Marina in Deauville

91

As Normandy has a tradition of horse-breeding, **riding** is a popular pastime. The Association Régionale de Tourisme Equestre, rue Villate, F-76200 Dieppe, tel: 35 84 29 48. There are several companies in the region which organise horse riding and rides in horse-drawn carriages. Contact: Ferme de Loisir, 76440 Mauquenchy, Pays de Bray, tel: 35 90 58 22, fax: 35 90 49 46. Brochures are also available from Comité Régional de Tourisme de Normandie, 14 rue Charles Corbeau, F-27000 Evreux, tel: 32 33 79 00, fax: 32 31 19 04.

A **cruise** on the Seine can add to the pleasure of a visit. Boats ply between Paris and Honfleur and passengers can leave or join at any of the intervening places. For more details contact Fleuves et Loisirs, 29 avenue Claude Monet, F-95510 Vetheuil, tel: 34 78 16 32, fax: 34 78 23 96. 'Le Normandie', a 53-berth hotel ship, takes six nights/seven days to cover the same route. Contact: Aqua Viva, quai de Grenelle, F-75015, tel: 45 75 52 60, fax: 45 75 52 31. Boat trips between Le Havre and Rouen (lunch included) are organised by 'Salamandre', M Fortin, BP 1086, F-76062 Le Havre, Cedex, tel: 35 42 01 31.

Kids love Normandy, too

The area southwest of Alençon is one where **ramblers** will find some splendid walks. For more details contact Maison du Parc, Parc Régional Normandie-Maine, F-61320 Carrouges, tel: 33 27 21 15.

Getting There

By plane

Air France flies direct to Paris from London and New York and other US cities. Travellers from America, however, may find it cheaper to take a charter flight to London, then go onward from there. Air France operates a rail package with flights available from a number of UK airports to Paris, then onward by train to the region. These inclusive tickets can also be combined with a rail pass. For schedules and booking, contact Air France. Brit Air offer services from Gatwick to Caen and Le Havre, bookable through Air France, as above. Régional Airlines offer flights from Gatwick to Rouen, also bookable through Air France.

In the UK: Air France, 177 Piccadilly, London W1. Tel: 0171-750 4306.

In the US: Air France, 666 Fifth Avenue, New York NY 10019, tel: 212-315 1122 (toll-free reservations: 1-800-237 2747); 8501 Wilshire Boulevard, Beverly Hills, Los Angeles, CA 90211, tel: 213-688 9220.

By ship

Several ferry services operate across the English Channel from the UK, Ireland and the Channel Islands to Normandy. All carry cars as well as foot passengers.

Brittany Ferries offer sailings from Portsmouth to Caen, and a slightly cheaper 'Les Routiers' service from Poole to Cherbourg (summer only). For details contact: The Brittany Centre, Wharf Road, Portsmouth PO2 8RU, tel: 01705-827701; or from Millbay Docks, Plymouth PL1 3EW, tel: 01752-221321.

The docks at Cherbourg

P & O European Ferries sail from Portsmouth to Cherbourg and Le Havre, and also operate the short sea route from Dover to Calais. Fares and schedules: P & O, Channel House, Channel View Road, Dover CT17 9TJ, tel: 01304-203388.

Stena Sealink Line operate between Southampton and Cherbourg and also offer the northern routes from Newhaven to Dieppe (which offers speedy access to Rouen) and Dover to Calais. Information and bookings: Charter House, Park Street, Ashford, Kent TN24 8EX, tel: 01233-643381.

By train

The Channel Tunnel offers fast, frequent Eurostar rail services between London (Waterloo) and Paris (Gare du Nord). France has a fast and efficient rail network operated by the SNCF (Société Nationale des Chemins de Fer de France). There are direct connections to the main cities of the region from Paris Saint-Lazare and Montparnasse stations. Paris to Rouen takes 1 hour 20 minutes, Paris-

Trains connect all the main cities

Caen 3 hours, Paris-Cherbourg 4 hours, Paris-Deauville 2 hours (for further details of rail connections, *see Places*).

Tickets may be booked for through journeys from outside France. In the UK tickets can be booked from any British Rail station, including ferry and Channel Tunnel travel. There are several rail-only and rail combination passes available to foreign visitors. These must always be bought before departing for France. In the UK a Eurodomino Pass offers unlimited rail travel on any 3, 5 or 10 days within a month. Visitors from North America have a wider choice of passes, starting with the basic France Railpass which offers four or nine days' unlimited travel within a month. Then there are various types of Eurail Pass which offer varying periods of first-class travel throughout Europe; the Eurail Youthpass offers a similar deal for young people under 26. The France Rail 'n' Drive Pass offers a flexible rail and car rental package, while the Fly Rail 'n' Drive Pass combines internal flights on Air Inter with train travel and car hire.

In the UK information and reservations for all the above services can be obtained from French Railways Ltd, 179 Piccadilly, London W1 0BA, tel: 0171-493 9731; special information line, tel: 01891-515477; reservations tel: 0171-495 4433. British Rail International Enquiries, International Rail Centre, Victoria Station, London SW1, tel: 0171-834 2345.

In the US contact Raileurope Inc. on their nationwide toll-free number 1-800-4-EURAIL or in **Canada** 1-800-361 7425.

By car

Normandy is an ideal destination for car travellers, with good motorways from Paris (N13 to Evreux and Caen, N14 to Rouen). The roads are good in the region, and reasonably uncrowded, except on the main routes to and from Paris at peak holiday times (the first and last weekends in August).

Journey's end

Almost all motorways in France are privately owned and subject to tolls (credit cards are usually accepted). A toll is also payable on the Brotonne Bridge and the Tancarville Bridge over the Seine, as well as the Pont de Normandie, the impressive new motorway bridge connecting Le Havre to Honfleur, which has improved access from the port to the coastal resorts of Deauville, Trouville etc. Caen centre is less than 30 minutes from the port of Ouistreham and Rouen is only about an hour away from the ports of Le Havre or Dieppe.

Le Shuttle, the Channel Tunnel service taking cars and their passengers from Folkestone to Calais on a drive-on-drive-off system, takes 35 minutes.

Getting Around

By train

Information on services is available from stations (*gare* SCNF). If you intend to travel extensively by train it may be worth obtaining a rail pass before leaving home (*see page 93*). Children under 4 travel free, from 4 to 12 for half-fare.

Train et Vélo: Bicycles can be hired from most main stations. On many trains, cycles can be transported free of charge in the luggage van. Free brochures on transporting cycles by train are available at all French stations.

By car

British, US, Canadian and Australian licences are all valid in France and you should always carry your vehicle's registration document and insurance (third party is the absolute minimum, and a green card is strongly recommended). The Automobile Club National will assist any motorist whose own club has an agreement with it. Contact them at 9 rue Anatole-de-la-Forge, 75017 Paris. Tel: (1) 42 27 82 00, fax: (1) 40 53 90 52.

Britons must remember to drive on the right and that priority on French roads is always given to vehicles approaching from the right. The minimum age for driving in France is 18; foreigners are not permitted to drive on a provisional licence. The use of seat belts and crash helmets for motorcyclists is compulsory. Children under 10 are not permitted to ride in the front seat unless fitted with a rear-facing safety seat, or if the car has no rear seat.

Speed limits are as follows, unless otherwise indicated: 80 mph (130 kph) on toll motorways; 68 mph (110 kph) on other motorways and dual carriageways; 56 mph (90 kph) on other roads except in towns where the limit is 30 mph (50 kph). There is a *minimum* speed limit of 50 mph (80 kph) on the outside lane of motorways during daylight with good visibility and on level ground. Speed limits are reduced in wet weather. In an accident or emergency, call the police (dial 17) or use the free emergency telephones on motorways.

Car hire

Some fly/drive deals work out reasonably well on short visits. French Railways offer a good deal on their combined train/car rental bookings. Weekly rates often work out better than a daily hire and it can be cheaper to arrange hire before leaving for France. Most companies will not hire to anyone under 23, or 21 if paying by credit card and the hirer must have held a full licence for at least a year. The major car hire companies have local offices in Normandy's main cities.

Discussing itineraries

In towns the speed limit is 50 kmph

95

Weekly rates often work out cheaper than daily hire

Facts for the Visitor

Visas

All visitors to France need a valid passport. No visa is currently required by visitors from any EU country or from the US, Canada or Japan. Nationals of other countries do require a visa. If in any doubt check with the French consulate in your country.

Enjoying the summer

Tourist information

The French Tourist Board can supply information and brochures on all regions of France.

In the UK: Maison de la France/French Government Tourist Office, 178 Piccadilly, London W1V 0AL, tel: 0171-491 7622, fax: 0171-493 6594.

In the US: Maison de la France/French Government Tourist Office, 610 Fifth Avenue, Suite 222, New York, NY 10020-2452, tel: 212-757 1125, fax: 212-247 6468; 9454 Wilshire Boulevard, Beverley Hills, Los Angeles CA 90212-2967, tel: 310-271 7838; 645 North Michigan Avenue, Suite 630, Chicago, Illinois 6061l-2836, tel: 312-337 6301.

In Paris: Maison de la France, 8 Avenue de l'Opéra, 75001 Paris. Tel: (1) 42 96 10 23.

In Normandy: Comité Régional de Tourisme de Normandie, 14 rue Charles Corbeau, F-27000 Evreux, tel: 32 33 79 00, fax: 32 31 19 04.

The following tourist offices are in the main towns covered in the Places section of this guide and can usually provide information about their region: **Caen**, Office du Tourisme, 14 place St-Pierre, tel: 31 27 14 18, fax: 31 27 14 11; Calvados Tourisme, Place du Canada, F-14000 Caen, tel: 31 86 53 30, fax: 31 79 39 41; **Cherbourg**, Office du Tourisme, F-50100 Cherbourg, 2 quai Alexandre III, tel: 33 93 52 02; **Dieppe**, Syndicat d'Initiative, Pont Jehan Ango, F-76200 Dieppe, tel: 35 84 11 77, fax: 35 06 27 66, closed Sunday. Information kiosk, Rotonde de la Plage, July and August only, tel: 35 84 28 70; **Evreux**, Office du Tourisme, Place du Général de Gaulle, F-27000, tel: 32 24 04 43; Comité Départemental de Tourisme de l'Eure, Hôtel du Département, Boulevard G. Chavin, tel: 32 31 51 51, fax: 32 31 05 98; **Le Havre**, Syndicat d'Initiative, Place de l'Hôtel de Ville, BP 649, F-76059 Le Havre, tel: 35 21 22 88, fax: 35 42 38 39; **Rouen**, Syndicat d'Initiative, 25 place de la Cathédrale, F-76000, tel: 35 71 41 77, fax: 35 98 55 50. Open Easter to end of October, Monday to Saturday 9am–7pm, Sunday and holidays 9.30am–12.30pm, 2.30–6pm; November to Easter, daily 9am–noon and 2.30–6.30pm, closed Sunday; **Suisse Normande**, Office du Tourisme, Place de l'Eglise, F-14570 Clécy, tel: 31 69 79 95; Office du Tourisme, Place

Dieppe Tourist Office

Rouen Tourist Office

Apples galore

de la Mairie, Condé-sur-Noir, tel: 31 69 27 64; Office du
Tourisme, Place St-Sauveur, F-14220 Thury-Harcourt, tel:
31 79 70 45.

Currency and exchange

Cash point

The main unit of currency is the French franc (FF), which
is divided into 100 centimes (c). Coins in circulation are
10, 5, 2, 1FF and 50, 20, 10, 5c. Notes are available in
the following denominations 500, 200, 100, 50, 20FF.

By using a Eurocheque card, cash can be withdrawn
from automatic teller machines outside normal banking
hours. A maximum of 1,400FF may be drawn with one
Eurocheque, but again a charge is levied.

Try to use up any notes or coins before leaving, as converting back to sterling or dollars can prove expensive.

If possible, take travellers' cheques in francs.

Credit cards are accepted in most hotels. Paying with
plastic cards may be a problem in the remoter rural regions.

Tipping

In restaurants and cafés a service charge is always included
in the price, but an additional tip is usually expected.

Opening times

There are no strict regulations for shop opening hours in
France. In general, shops and banks in country areas stay
open for shorter periods than branches in town.
Banks
9am–12noon and 2–4pm, closed Saturday and Monday.
Shops
Shops are normally open 8am–12noon and 2–7pm.
Many of the hypermarkets are open 9am–9pm, but they
often open later on Monday at either noon or 1pm.
Official Offices
Monday to Friday, 9am–12noon and 2–5pm.

Post offices

The PTT Post Offices *(Administration des Postes Télé-graphes et Téléphones)* and P et T *(Ministère des Postes et Télécommunications)* are open from Monday to Friday 9am–7pm (in country areas Monday to Friday 8am–12noon and 2–6.30pm) and on Saturday until noon.
Museums
Most state-run museums are closed on Monday or Tuesday and between noon and 2pm. There are no fixed opening times for smaller museums. Ask at the *Syndicat d'Initiative* or *Office de Tourisme*.

A slice of Normandy

Postal services

Stamps *(timbres)* are available from post offices, tobacconists *(tabac)* and bars which sell cigarettes *(bar-tabac)*.

Souvenirs

The best souvenirs from Normandy can be either eaten or drunk. If the journey home is not too long, then some fresh cheese from one of the weekly markets makes a welcome present. A bottle of Calvados will survive the journey home more easily and is sure to be well received.

Check the children's clothes sizes

Clothes sizes

Most shops will let you try on clothes *(essayer)* before buying. Children's sizes, in particular, tend to be small compared with UK and US age ranges. Hypermarkets have good-value children's clothes.

Public holidays

New Year's Day, Easter Monday, 1 May (Labour Day), 8 May (VE Day), Ascension Day, Whit Monday, 14 July (Bastille Day), 15 August (Assumption of the Virgin Mary), 1 November (All Saints), 11 November (Armistice Day 1918), 25 December (Christmas Day).

Telephone

Have a card handy

More card-operated telephones are likely to be found than the old coin-operated models. Post offices and *tabacs* sell the plastic cards with 50 or 120 units. A local call costs 1FF and the cheap tariff for long-distance calls applies on weekdays from 6pm to 8am, Saturday from 2pm to 8am on Monday and on public holidays. The cheap rate for calls abroad starts at 9.30pm.

Calling from one *département* to another requires no dialling code for 8-digit numbers, other then a 1 for Paris.

To make an international call, lift the receiver, insert the money (if necessary), dial 19, wait for the tone to change, then dial the country code, followed by the area code (omitting any initial 0) and the number. AT&T, tel: 19-0011; MCI, tel: 19-0019; Sprint, tel: 19-0087.

To take advantage of cheap rates, use the telephone weekdays between 10.30pm and 8am and at weekends after 2pm on Saturday.

Time
French time is one hour ahead of Greenwich Mean Time, six hours ahead of Eastern Standard Time.

One hour ahead

Voltage
Apart from one or two exceptions, mains voltage is 220V. It is worth buying an adapter for continental sockets if you are intending to take any electrical appliances.

Medical
Visitors to France can expect to have to pay for medical treatment, should it be necessary. Although travellers from EU countries are advised to acquire the E111 certificate, which entitles holders to take advantage of health facilities in other EU countries, in practice not all doctors will accept it, preferring to make private arrangements with patients. It is much safer to take out ordinary travel insurance which generally meets the full extent of any claim.

For minor ailments it may be worth consulting a pharmacy (recognisable by its green cross sign), who have wider 'prescribing' powers than chemists in the UK or US. Emergency opening times for chemists *(pharmacies)* are usually published in the local newspapers, sometimes in the tourist offices *(Syndicat d'Initiative or Office de Tourisme)* but are always on display at the chemist's shop.

In cases of medical emergency, either dial 15 for an ambulance or call the Service d'Aide Médicale d'Urgence (SAMU) which exists in most large towns and cities – numbers are given at the front of telephone directories.

Emergencies
Ambulance: tel: 15
Police: tel: 17.
Fire *(sapeurs-pompiers)*: tel: 18

The disabled
A list of accommodation which is suitable for the disabled can be obtained from the A.P.F., Délégation de Paris, 22 rue du Père-Guérin, F-75013 Paris.

Newspapers
Newspapers can be bought at kiosks, bookshops or in *bartabacs*. There are some regional newspapers such as *Paris-Normandie*, *Ouest-France* or *Presse de la Manche*. Foreign newspapers are available from good newsagents and bookshops.

Read all about it

Hotel Beuron en Auge

Accommodation

The choice varies from a historic castle or luxury hotel to private rooms in a farmhouse. Most hotels are accredited by the *Direction du Tourisme* and there are five different categories. Hotels which have been approved by the tourist office can be identified by the hexagonal blue plate showing the letter 'H' at the entrance. The number of stars on the plate indicates the degree of comfort and also the price range.

In this guide, the first three categories are shown under the heading FFF, FF and F in descending order of expense. A number of hotels, holiday homes and private rooms are not approved by the local tourist board and hence are not classified. A list of all hotels in the region can be obtained from the following address: Comité Régional de Tourisme de Normandie, 14 rue Charles Corbeau, F-27000 Evreux, tel: 32 33 79 00, fax: 32 31 19 04.

The Grand Hotel, Cabourg

Castles and stately homes

There is wide choice available to those who wish to spend the night in opulent surroundings. Converted castles and former stately homes are usually to be found some way off the beaten track.

Relais et Châteaux, 9 avenue Marceau, F-75116 Paris, tel: (1) 47 23 41 42, fax: (1) 47 23 38 99. In the UK: 7 Cork Street, London W1X 1PB, tel: 0171-491 2516.

Climat de France

These two-star hotels are geared towards families.

Climat de France, 5 Avenue du Cap-Horn, ZAC de Courtaboeuf, BP 93, 91943 Les Ulis, tel: (1) 64 46 01 23 or 05 11 22 11 (toll-free in France), fax: (1) 69 28 24 02. UK office: tel: 0171-287 3181.

Logis de France

The hotels in this group with its distinctive symbol of a yellow fireplace on a green background are usually smaller, family-run concerns, mainly located in country areas. Association des Logis de France de Normandie, 83 avenue d'Italie, F-75013 Paris, tel: (1) 45 84 83 84.

Relais du Silence

Expect to find these hotels in delightful, peaceful surroundings. The hoteliers are committed to providing high quality regional dishes.

Secretariat Relais du Silence, 2 passage du Guesclin, F-75015 Paris, tel: (1) 45 66 77 77, fax: (1) 40 65 90 09.

Holiday homes

Gîtes Ruraux are holiday houses or flats, usually set in the country. The organisation of the same name monitors the quality of the accommodation. UK booking office: 178 Piccadilly, London W1V 9DB, tel: 0171-493 3480

Chambres d'Hôtes are private houses which provide simple and cheap overnight accommodation similar to English 'Bed and Breakfast'. The standard of the accommodation is graded with stars (from * to ***).

Chambres d'Hotes

CHAMBRE D'HÔTES

Ferme-auberges

These privately-run inns can be found all over Normandy and most offer overnight accommodation. Their menus will usually contain regional specialities and locally-produced drinks. Many of these establishments belong to the Gîtes de France organisation (see above).

Youth hostels

A full list of youth hostels in Normandy can be obtained from your local Youth Hostel Association. An international youth hostel card should be obtained before departure. There are two different organisations in France:

Fédération Unie des Auberges de Jeunesse, 27 rue Pajol, F-75018 Paris, tel: (1) 46 07 00 01, fax: (1) 46 07 93 10. *Ligue Française pour les Auberges de la Jeunesse*, 38 boulevard Raspail, F-75007 Paris, tel: (1) 45 48 69 84, fax: (1) 45 44 57 47.

In addition, there are international centres, which are run by the Union de Rencontres Internationales de France, 21 rue Béranger, F-75003 Paris. These hostels are affiliated to the one or other of the youth hostel organisations.

Camping and caravans

During the high season advance booking on official sites is recommended. A full list of camp sites in the region is available at all tourist offices. Alternatively, Michelin publish an annual guide to camp and caravan sites.

Book your space in advance

Fine dining in the Relais des Gourmets

The Holiday Inn

Bayeux

FFF **Lion d'Or**, 71 rue St-Jean, tel: 31 92 06 90, fax: 31 22 15 64. A luxury town-centre hotel in an historic old building; **Luxembourg**, 25 rue Bouchers, tel: 31 92 00 04, fax: 31 92 54 26. A comfortable hotel in a central location.

FF **Argouges**, 21 rue St-Patrice, tel: 31 92 88 86, fax: 31 21 41 66. Well above average accommodation, on the edge of the old town; **Churchill**, 14-16 rue St-Jean, tel: 31 21 31 80, fax: 31 21 41 66. Good terms for half board.

F **Reine Mathilde**, 23 rue Larcher, tel: 31 92 08 13. A small, simple, centrally located hotel.

Caen

FFF **Relais des Gourmets**, 13-15 rue de Geôle, tel: 31 86 06 01, fax: 31 39 06 00. The finest hotel in town situated near the old castle. **Holiday Inn Hotel**, Place Foch, tel: 31 27 57 57, fax 31 27 57 58. On the southern side of the city near the racetrack.

FF **Hôtel de France**, 10 rue de la Gare, tel: 31 52 16 99, fax: 31 83 23 16. Special facilities for the handicapped.

F **Quatrans** 17 rue Gemare, tel: 31 86 25 57, fax: 31 85 27 80. A central location but in a side street; **Central** 23 place J. Letellier, tel: 31 86 18 52, fax: 31 86 88 11. Not far from the tourist office in the city centre.

Cherbourg

FFF **Quality Hotel**, Rue G.-Sorel, tel: 33 43 72 00, fax: 33 43 72 06. Pleasant atmosphere and nice rooms away from the town centre; **Hôtel Mercure**, Gare Maritime, tel: 33 44 01 11, fax: 33 44 51 00. Opposite ferry terminal.

FF **Chantereyne**, Port de Plaisance, tel: 33 93 02 20, fax: 33 93 45 29. Swimming pool and marina nearby.

Dieppe

FFF **Aguado**, 30 boulevard de Verdun, tel: 35 84 27 00, fax: 35 06 17 61. A comfortable hotel only a few yards from the beach; **La Présidence**, 2 boulevard de Verdun, tel: 35 84 31 31, fax: 35 84 86 70. Close to the casino

FF **Plage**, 20 boulevard de Verdun, tel: 35 84 18 28, fax: 35 82 36 82. Many rooms with sea view; **Epsom**, 11 boulevard de Verdun, tel: 35 84 10 18, fax: 35 40 03 00. A pleasant, refined atmosphere.

Deauville

FFF **Normandy**, 38 rue Jean-Mermoz, tel: 31 98 66 22, fax: 31 98 66 23. Luxury accommodation in ornate half-timbered-style building; **Du Golf**, Mt Canisy, tel: 31 88 19 01, fax: 31 88 75 99. Expensive hotel with wide range of sporting facilities; **Royal**, Boulevard Cornuché, tel: 31 98 66 33, fax: 31 98 66 34. Well-managed, well-equipped and very expensive.

FF **Continental**, 1 rue Désiré le Hoc, tel: 31 88 21 06, fax: 31 98 93 67. Comfortable accommodation; **Hélios**, 10 rue R. Fossorier, tel: 31 88 28 26, fax: 31 88 53 87. Central location.

Evreux
FFF **Mercure**, Boulevard de Normandie, tel: 32 38 77 77, fax: 32 39 04 53. Evreux's finest hotel with all facilities.

FF **Normandy** 31 rue Eduard-Féray, tel: 32 33 14 40, fax: 32 31 24 74. A comfortable hotel on the northern edge of the town centre; **L'Orme**, 13 rue des Lombards, tel: 32 39 34 12, fax: 23 33 62 48. In the heart of the town.

F **Gambetta**, 61 boulevard Gambetta, tel: 32 33 37 71, fax: 32 33 37 82. Near the public parks.

Hôtel Normandy, Evreux

Le Havre
FFF **Hôtel de Bordeaux**, 147 rue L. Brindeau, tel: 35 22 69 44, fax: 35 42 09 27. All of the sights in the town centre are within easy walking distance; **Mercure**, Chaussée d'Angoulême, tel: 35 19 50 50, fax: 35 19 50 99. A fine hotel, probably the best equipped in the city.

FF **Hôtel Marly**, 121 rue de Paris, tel: 35 41 72 48, fax: 35 21 50 45. An elegant hotel between the port and cultural centre; **Hôtel Foch**, 4 rue Caligny, tel: 35 42 50 69, fax: 35 43 40 17. Central location.

F **Le Green**, 209 boulevard de Strasbourg, tel: 35 22 63 10, fax 35 22 57 62. Clean but no frills; **Bauza**, 15 rue G. Braque, tel: 35 42 27 27, fax: 35 42 13 67. Close to the Place de l'Hôtel de Ville.

Mont St-Michel
FFF **St-Pierre et Logis du Chapeau Blanc**, tel: 33 60 14 03, fax: 33 48 59 82. A small but elegant hotel; **Digue**, tel: 33 60 14 02, fax: 33 60 37 59. Situated on the mainland not far from the causeway.

FF **Mouton Blanc**, tel: 33 60 14 08, fax: 33 60 05 62. Inside the walls of Mont St-Michel.

Rouen
FFF **Mercure-Champ de Mars**, avenue Aristide-Briand, tel: 35 52 42 32, fax: 35 08 15 06. A very clean 3-star hotel only a short distance from St-Maclou church; **Colin's Hotel**, 15 rue de la Pie, tel: 35 71 00 88, fax: 35 70 75 94. In the old town, with business facilities; **Le Manoir de St-Adrien**, 6 chemin de la Source, St-Adrien (south of Rouen), tel: 35 23 32 00, fax: 35 23 66 66. An elegant and very peaceful half-timbered country house.

FF **Versan**, 3 rue Thiers, tel: 35 70 22 00, fax: 35 70 22 60 is well situated for the museums and St-Ouen church.

F **Viking**, 21 quai du Havre, tel: 35 70 34 95, fax: 35 89 97 12. A friendly hotel on the banks of the Seine.

Index